WHITEWORK
INSPIRATIONS

SEARCH PRESS

Introduction

Refined elegant designs, subtle monochromatic patterns, intriguingly intricate stitches – whitework is a technique that is as spectacular as it is timeless.

For over 30 years *Inspirations* magazine has been publishing the world's most beautiful needlework, during which time we have featured some superb whitework designs created by some very talented designers.

Now, for the very first time, we have put together this special collection of 8 projects, specifically chosen to highlight the very best whitework has to offer in both design and technique.

Whitework is a general term used to define any embroidery worked with white or light-coloured thread onto white or light-coloured fabric and examples of this style of stitching can be found in many cultures across the world.

Without the addition of colour, the fabric surface is ornamented with high-relief stitching, cutting, pulling or withdrawing threads with some styles utilizing all these techniques. Much of the impact is dependant on the way light plays across the stitching, creating areas of light and shadow that emphasize the intricate designs.

If you're new to whitework, Heart's Delight by Kim Beamish is a great place to start, dainty in size and utilizing pulled thread techniques that don't require any cutting. Sweet Strawberry by Deborah Love, worked in the Irish Mountmellick style and Vintage, a Casalguidi bag by Judy Stephenson, demonstrate just how effective surface contrast can be.

Piercing and cutting the fabric can be used to create various effects and the beautiful Hedebo Tulip design by Christine P. Bishop and dainty broderie anglaise and Madeira sachets, Affair of the Heart and A Fine Romance by Susan O'Connor are delightful examples of these whitework styles.

If you are looking for something a little more challenging and on a larger scale, Patricia Girolami's wonderful Hardanger mat Bianca would be an ideal choice or perhaps Sense of Place by Luzine Happel, a superb Schwalm cloth will appeal. Both demonstrate the truly magical qualities of whitework and the spectacular results that can be achieved working with a single colour.

Every project comes complete with detailed instructions and step-by-step illustrations, plus a comprehensive list of all 59 stitches used across the 8 projects is also included in a special Stitch Guide at the back of this book, to help you learn and master every aspect of whitework.

Design outlines and construction information can be found on the pullout pattern sheets.

Whether you are a curious novice or a self-confessed whitework addict, we're so glad you've joined us, as together, we make the world more beautiful one stitch at a time.

Contents

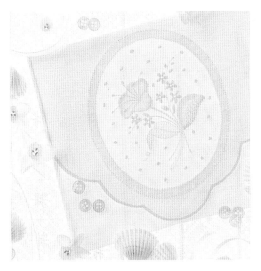

Whitework History

Rather than referring to one specific technique, whitework is a general term encompassing numerous embroidery styles that all share one characteristic, the use of white thread on white fabric. With a history dating back to the ancient Egyptians, whitework has been practised in some form in every age in most civilisations, resulting in a vast collection of diverse techniques from all corners of the globe.

Much of the appeal of whitework lies in the subtlety of the stitched surface and regardless of the materials and techniques used, its understated elegance allowed it to take centre stage or work as a support act to other more vibrantly coloured stitching, depending on the fashion of the time. In clothing, whitework could be found decorating undergarments, on a smock or chemise, peeping out at the neck or sleeve, the perfect foil for the rich, heavy fabrics and polychrome embroidery used to decorate outer garments. It was popular for household linen, nightgowns and nightshirts, baby garments, children's clothing, bonnets, coifs and aprons. These were all uses that required one thing that stood whitework apart from other textiles and made it so popular and widely utilized – the need and ability to be laundered.

Early washing techniques were brutal and uncompromising and laundry was not done very often.

Coarse lye soap made from wood ash and animal fat, boiling water and harsh rubbing and pounding were used to clean fabrics that were then laid out over grass in the sunshine to bleach and dry. Lye is a powerful bleach and white embroidery worked onto linen cloth could tolerate this treatment time and time again, unlike any coloured cloth. Early dyes were often unstable and linen had a tendency to fade badly, a characteristic that was an advantage in whitework. Rich silks and satins could not be washed and coloured embroidery could run, ruining the ground fabric. Using white fabrics for undergarments, linens and children's clothing that could be laundered at least allowed fresh, clean fabric next to the skin.

Having established its value and cemented its appeal, whitework techniques evolved according to the changing tastes and habits of the populace. Early in the 18th century the availability of fine linen threads had inspired lace makers to create superb examples of their craft. Expensive and extravagant, governments placed heavy duties on lace so skilled needleworkers looked for ways to imitate lace with embroidery. On fine linen cambric or Indian muslin, stitches were used to imitate lace fillings, worked under tension to pull the fabric threads together.

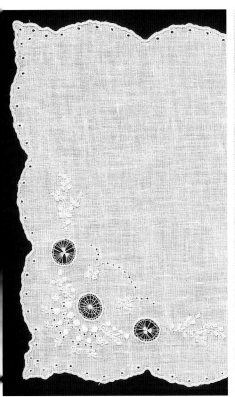

This early form of pulled thread embroidery was the basis for Dresden work. Much of this style of embroidery was professionally worked but the skills required were not beyond any competent needleworker and many examples survive that were stitched in the home.

Fashions changed and there was a demand for delicate whitework on a more substantial cloth than the soft fabrics used for Dresden embroidery. Muslin mills in Scotland produced a firmer cloth and Ayrshire embroidery came to the fore with its delicate, finely stitched floral motifs and dainty needlepoint lace fillings. Demand for this new style of embroidery was enormous and it developed into a commercial industry with work sent to other parts of Scotland and Northern Ireland to be completed. By the 1860s a form of cutwork known as broderie anglaise had surpassed Ayrshire as the most fashionable embroidery style and of all the whitework techniques, this one has proved the most enduring. Consisting primarily of cut and pierced eyelets worked in floral or geometric designs, the embroidery was worked onto firm calico or linen and used for petticoats, baby and children's clothing, and household linen.

At around the same time, a cottage embroidery industry was growing on the island of Madeira. Part of Portugal but 800km off the west coast of Africa, Madeira was famous for its wine and the daughter of an English wine importer noticed that the women were proficient with a needle and thread. She introduced Ayrshire and broderie anglaise techniques and vast quantities of Madeira embroidery were exported around the world.

In Ireland, Mountmellick embroidery was developed in the small town of the same name and the robust, heavy cotton stitching on a satin jean ground captured the beauty of the local flora perfectly. Focusing on bold surface embroidery, Mountmellick work is unlike any other whitework technique with textured stitches leaving as little thread as possible passing on the back. Created for use in the household, tablecloths, coverlets, cushion covers and pillow shams were stitched and it was also used to embellish Christening gowns.

In other parts of Europe unique whitework styles were also evolving and flourishing, sometimes in relatively closed communities where stitching was worked primarily for the use of the embroiderer and her family. Dating back to the 16th century, Danish Hedebo embroidery changed several times in style before its final incarnation became popular in other parts of the world. Schwalm embroidery from Germany developed in the mid-18th century and is thought to have originated as an imitation of popular Dresden work. Norwegian Hardanger, like many other embroidery styles, developed from ancient Persian embroidery, and was originally worked on 50-count linen, a far cry from the 22-count that is widely used today. In the late 19th century Casalguidi embroidery enjoyed a resurgence in the small Italian town that shares its name and these are but a few of the many whitework techniques that exist around the world.

Rich with imagery and a profusion of stitch techniques, whitework offers the embroiderer an inspiring journey through history and across cultures.

The
Whitework
Projects

Affair of the Heart

SUSAN O'CONNOR

The finest white linen fabric, pure cotton thread and a few stolen hours of heavenly stitching combine in this exquisite sachet. The dainty eyelets and perfectly stitched satin outlines form an elegant floral design in the broderie anglaise style. Padded blanket stitch finishes the decorative scalloped lower edge.

BEFORE YOU BEGIN

Read the complete instructions and pullout pattern

See the pullout pattern for the embroidery design

All embroidery is worked with ONE strand of thread

THIS DESIGN USES

Cut eyelet / Eyelet

Granitos / Line of pierced eyelets

Padded blanket stitch

Satin outline

**The finished sachet measures
16 x 19cm wide (6¼ x 7½in)**

REQUIREMENTS

Fabric

30 x 60cm wide
(12 x 24in) piece of fine
white evenweave linen

Supplies

Sewing awl or stiletto

Sharp HB pencil

Fine black pen

Tracing paper

Needle

No. 8 crewel

Thread

DMC Broder Spécial 25
blanc

Whitework, in its many guises, has always been one of the most popular styles of embroidery. In the early 19th century, fine cottons and muslins, exquisitely embroidered in a style known as Ayrshire work, were hugely popular. Changes in fashion led to a decline in the popularity of fine, delicate handwork for adult clothing but it retained its popularity for children's and babies' wear. Although very beautiful, Ayrshire embroidery was usually professionally worked and expensive to buy so when a new style of whitework, known as broderie anglaise, was introduced it quickly usurped Ayrshire as the most fashionable form of embroidered decoration.

Broderie anglaise is a French term that simply means English embroidery and it is characterised by the extensive use of eyelets and shaped blanket stitch edges. An eyelet is a hole in the fabric that is surrounded by overcasting stitches and can be made by piercing the cloth with a dressmaker's awl or stiletto, or by cutting.

Early examples used eyelets exclusively to create ornate patterns that often closely resembled lace. As the style gained popularity, other surface embroidery techniques were introduced, reducing the number of eyelets and making it quicker to work. Broderie anglaise is much coarser in appearance

than Ayrshire but it had the advantage of being much simpler to stitch and could be worked in the home by any competent needlewoman.

Hugely popular for children's and baby garments, hand worked broderie anglaise was also used extensively as a trimming for ladies' clothing, nightwear and household linens. It enjoyed a long period of popularity and was being used on petticoat hems into the 20th century. The advent of machine embroidery has meant that broderie anglaise is still available today, both as edgings and as fabric yardage and it is currently undergoing another surge in popularity in ladies' clothing.

PREPARATION FOR EMBROIDERY

PREPARING THE FABRIC

Lightly spray the fabric with starch, allowing 60 seconds for it to soak in, then press. Repeat this process three or four times until the fabric is firm.

TRANSFERRING THE DESIGN

Using the black pen, trace the design, scalloped outline and placement marks onto the tracing paper. With the right side facing up, place the linen over the tracing, matching the straight grain and the placement mark below the design with one short edge of the fabric. Tape in place. Using the pencil, lightly trace the design and scalloped outline onto the fabric.

EMBROIDERY

See pages 15–17 for step-by-step instructions for working an eyelet, a cut eyelet, line of pierced eyelets and satin outline.

Refer to the close-up photograph for stitch placement.

Use the no. 8 crewel needle and DMC Broder spécial thread for all embroidery.

ORDER OF WORK

DAISY

Embroider eyelets at the centre of the three daisies and work the petals with cut eyelets, following the step-by-step instructions. Stitch the stems with a row of satin outline for each. Embroider the leaves along the stems, working cut eyelets in the same manner as the daisy petals.

DECORATIVE ARC

Stitch the decorative arc above the daisies, working a row of pierced eyelets, following the step-by-step instructions.

TRAIL

Embroider the trail of granitos at the marked positions, working over the stitches until the desired thickness

and coverage are achieved. Gradually reduce the size of the granitos towards the outer edges of the design.

> "Traditionally, these small dots would have been worked with padded satin stitch but granitos are a much quicker way to work a satin dot. Wrap the fabric over the index finger when working these, to give a fuller shape."
>
> SUSAN

SCALLOPED EDGE

Stitch the scalloped edge of the design with padded blanket stitch. Leaving a tail of thread, work long running

stitches along the straight edge of the sachet front (diag 1).

Continue the running stitch along the scalloped edge, taking as few stitches as possible (diag 2).

Stitch the remaining straight edge of the sachet in the same manner, leaving a tail at the end. Add more rows of padding for the required depth. Beginning on the left-hand side, work blanket stitch over the padding. Snip away the padding thread tails (diag 3).

CONSTRUCTION

See the pullout pattern.

EYELET

These embroidered eyelets are the basis of traditional white-on-white broderie anglaise or Swiss embroideries. They are also used in Madeira and Venetian embroidery. An eyelet is a pierced hole that is surrounded by running stitches, then covered by short, regular overcasting stitches. The beauty of this technique is in the regularity of the stitches.

1 Mark a tiny circle on the fabric. Leaving a short tail, work a row of running stitches around the circle, leaving tiny stitches at the back.

2 Work a split stitch through the first stitch in the circle, then bring the thread to the front just outside the outline at A.

3 Trim the tail close to the fabric. Using an awl, pierce the fabric and open up the eyelet.

4 Take the needle down through the hole and emerge on the outer edge. Pull the thread firmly.

EYELET

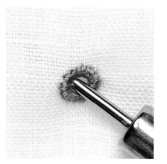

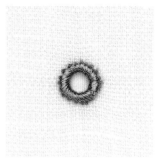

5 Continue working overcast stitches until two stitches from completing the circle. Work the final two stitches leaving them loose.

6 Take the needle through the two stitches and pull firmly. Snip the thread close to the stitching.

7 Using the awl, re-pierce the eyelet from the front and back. This helps to settle the thread and fabric.

8 Finished eyelet.

CUT EYELET

These eyelets are stitched in a similar manner to the pierced eyelets, however the fabric is cut rather than pierced.

1 Work a split stitch through the first stitch then bring the thread to the surface outside the outline.

2 Trim the tail close to the fabric. Using small sharp scissors, carefully cut the fabric into quarters at the centre of the shape.

3 Using the needle or the awl, fold each quarter of fabric under before beginning to overcast the section.

4 Complete the overcasting, trimming any excess fabric on the back. Secure the thread in the same manner as the pierced eyelet.

LINE OF PIERECED EYELETS

Use this method when you require a trail of eyelets. When working the first pass of overcasting stitches, skip across the point where the two circles touch. Stitch this when returning with the second pass of overcasting. This prevents having an unsightly lump of thread if this point is overcast twice.

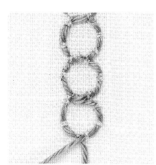

1 Work a line of running stitches around the outline in the shape of a figure eight.

2 Using the awl, pierce each eyelet before working the first edge.

3 Work the overcast stitches following the same path as the running stitches.

4 Complete the overcasting before securing the thread in the same manner as the pierced eyelet.

SATIN OUTLINE

Used in French whitework where it is known as cordonnet, satin outline is similar to trailing but is usually consistent in height and width, so there are no threads added or subtracted. It is worked along a single design line. When worked over a thicker line of stitching it is known as point de bourdon or bourdon stitch.

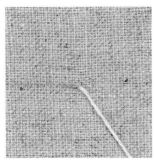

1 Secure the thread and bring it to the front at the beginning of the line.

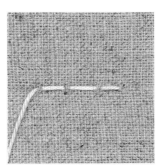

2 Work running stitches along the design line taking only 1–2 threads of fabric when making a stitch.

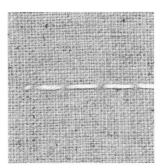

3 Continue working in this manner to the end of the line. You should have long stitches on the top of the fabric and tiny stitches on the back.

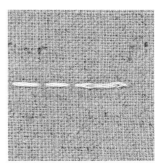

4 Bring the thread to the front at the centre of the first stitch. Take the thread to the back just before the centre of the second stitch, splitting the stitch.

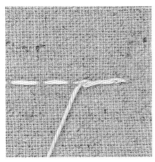

5 Bring the thread to the front just beyond the centre of the second stitch, again splitting the stitch. Pick up only 1–2 threads of fabric with this stitch.

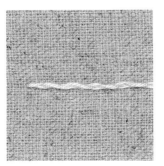

6 Repeat steps 4 and 5, working in this manner to the end of the line.

7 Cut a thread 5cm (2in) longer than the line. Ensure this 'guide' rests on top of the padding, without being attached, when working the satin stitch.

8 Beginning with a new thread, work satin stitches over the padding and guide, angling the needle as it passes through the fabric, to maintain a fine line.

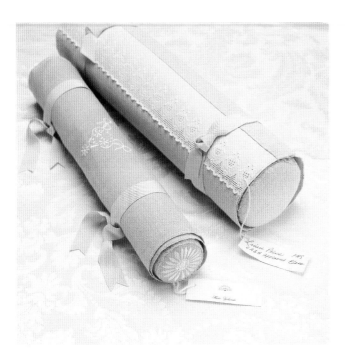

Heart's Delight

KIM BEAMISH

Pulled thread embroidery can magically transform a plain piece of fabric into the most delicate lace with nothing more than a needle and thread. Working carefully placed stitches and tensioning them firmly distorts the fabric weave, opening up holes and altering the angle of the embroidery stitches to create a vast array of beautiful patterns.

THIS DESIGN USES

Blanket stitch / Diagonal drawn filling
Framed cross filling / Honeycomb filling
Outline stitch / Single faggot filling
Waffle filling

**The finished mat measures
16.5cm (6½in) square**

REQUIREMENTS

Fabric

30cm (12in) square of antique white 28-count evenweave linen

Supplies

20cm (8in) embroidery hoop

Light-coloured sewing thread

Sharp embroidery scissors

Needles

No. 22 tapestry

No. 24 tapestry

Threads

DMC no. 8 perlé cotton
A = blanc
DMC no. 12 perlé cotton
B = blanc

PREPARATION FOR EMBROIDERY

PREPARING THE FABRIC

Neaten the raw edges of the linen with a machine zigzag or overlock stitch to prevent fraying. Using the sewing thread, work lines of tacking over and under four threads to mark the vertical and horizontal centres of the fabric (diag 1).

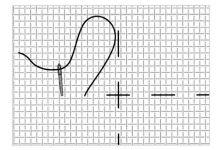

TRANSFERRING THE DESIGN

The design can be worked by following the graph only but if you prefer, each section can be marked onto the fabric with an erasable fabric pen or by tacking along the design lines using the light-coloured sewing thread.

A perfect introduction to the delights of this timeless technique, this sweet little mat utilizes five easily worked pulled thread stitches to fill a variety of large, small and medium hearts. Worked with two weights of perlé cotton onto antique white linen, the dainty mat is finished with a neat blanket stitch edge.

EMBROIDERY

See this page for the embroidery chart and pages 24–27 for step-by-step instructions for working framed cross filling, waffle filling, single faggot filling, diagonal drawn filling and honeycomb filling.

Refer to the embroidery chart for stitch placement.

Use the no. 22 tapestry needle for the no. 8 perlé cotton and the no. 24 tapestry needle for the no. 12 perlé cotton.

Work the pulled thread stitches in the hoop and the blanket stitch edge in the hand.

CHART

One square is equal to 2 x 2 fabric threads.

ORDER OF WORK

OUTER BORDER

Following the chart, embroider the outer border with blanket stitch using **A**. The stitches are worked one fabric thread apart and four fabric threads deep.

INNER OUTLINES

Embroider the inner outlines with outline stitch using **A**. If used, remove the outline tacking as you work.

FILLING

Each section is worked with a pulled thread filling as indicated below using **B**.

Section one: Honeycomb filling
Section two: Waffle filling
Section three: Diagonal drawn filling
Section four: Framed cross filling
Section five: Single faggot filling

HINT

Pulled thread stitches

Pull the threads firmly enough to create the decorative holes, but take care not to pucker the fabric.

FINISHING

Carefully cut away the excess fabric from the outer edge of the design, cutting as close as possible to the edge of the blanket stitch border and angling the scissors under the beaded edge of the blanket stitch.

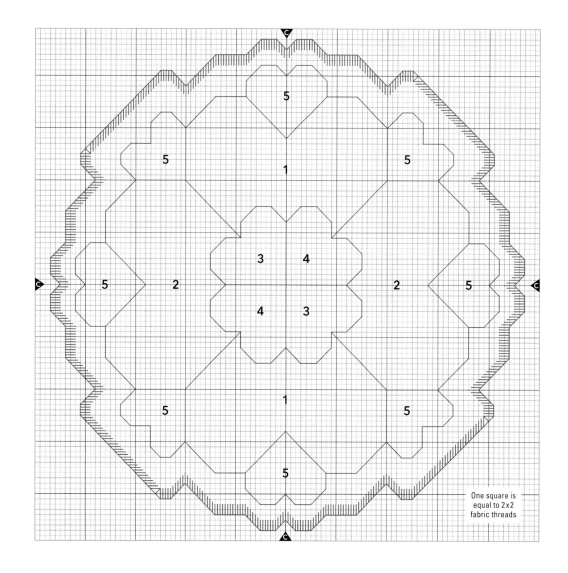

One square is equal to 2x2 fabric threads

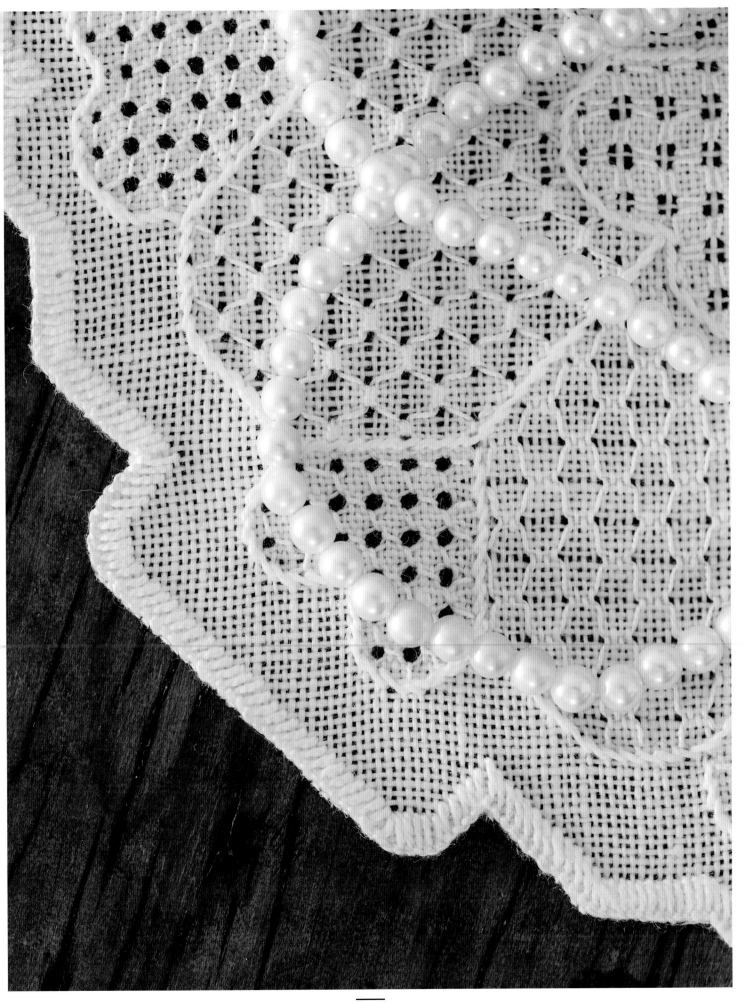

FRAMED CROSS FILLING

Pairs of satin stitches worked in horizontal and vertical rows open out holes in the fabric with crosses formed from single fabric threads. Each stitch is worked over four fabric threads.

1 Horizontal rows. Work pairs of vertical satin stitches across the first row, leaving four fabric threads between each pair.

2 Leave one horizontal fabric thread. Work pairs of vertical satin stitches back across the row, aligning the stitches with the previous row.

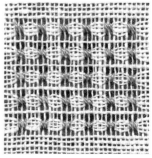

3 Work horizontal rows until the shape is full.

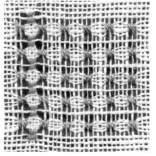

4 Vertical rows. Working from the upper to the lower edge, stitch pairs of horizontal satin stitches between the previous stitches.

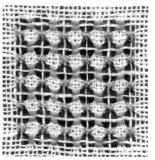

5 Continue working pairs of horizontal stitches down the remaining vertical rows to complete the filling.

DIAGONAL DRAWN FILLING

This filling is worked in a similar manner to single faggot filling, with one fabric thread left between diagonal rows of stitching rather than fabric holes being shared between rows. This leaves a delicate cross of fabric threads within the opened holes created by the pulled stitches. Each stitch is worked over four fabric threads.

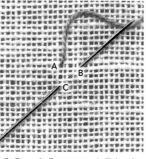

1 Row 1. Emerge at A. Take the needle from B to C.

2 Pull the thread taut. Take the needle from A to D.

3 Pull the thread taut. Take the needle from C to E.

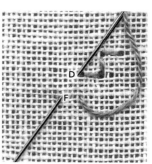

4 Pull the thread taut. Take the needle from D to F.

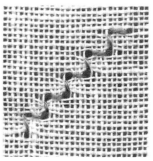

5 Pull the thread taut. Repeat the stitch sequence to the end of the row.

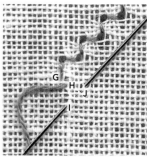

6 Row 2. Emerge at H, one thread across and down from G. Take the needle from I to J.

7 Pull the thread taut. Take the needle from H to L.

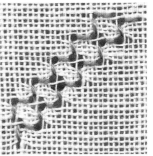

8 Pull the thread taut. Repeat the stitch sequence along the diagonal, in the opposite direction to row 1.

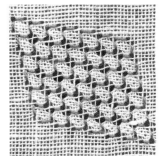

9 Continue working diagonal rows of diagonal drawn filling until the shape is filled, working partial rows where needed.

SINGLE FAGGOT FILLING

This stitch is worked diagonally and opens out an evenly spaced grid of holes across the fabric. Work the first row across the widest point of the shape and fill to one side, then complete the remaining side.
Each row shares fabric holes with the previous row. Each stitch is worked over four fabric threads.

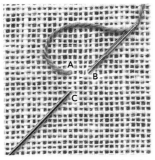

1 **Row 1.** Emerge at A. Take the needle from B to C.

2 Pull the thread taut. Take the needle from A to D, four fabric threads to the left of B and C.

3 Pull the thread taut. Take the needle from C to E.

4 Pull the thread taut. Take the needle from D to F.

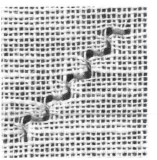

5 Pull the thread taut. Repeat the stitch sequence to the end of the row.

6 **Row 2.** Emerge at G. Take the needle from H to I.

7 Pull the thread taut. Take the needle through the holes created by the previous row as shown.

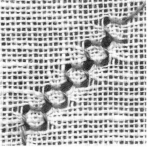

8 Pull the thread taut. Continue working stitches in the same manner along the diagonal, in the opposite direction to row 1.

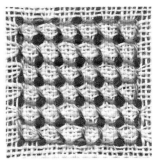

9 Continue working diagonal rows of single faggot filling to complete the shape, working partial rows where needed.

HONEYCOMB FILLING

This filling stitch creates a similar lattice to waffle stitch, with a horizontal backstitch being worked between the vertical stitches creating a more formal texture. The tension of the pulled stitching causes the vertical stitches to lie on the diagonal. Each stitch is worked over four fabric threads.

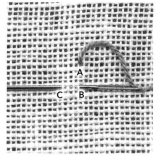

1 Beginning at the right-hand side, emerge at A. Take the needle from B to C.

2 Pull the thread through. Take the needle from B to C a second time.

3 Pull the thread through firmly to form a backstitch, pulling the fabric threads together.

4 Take the needle from D to E.

5 Pull the thread through. Take the thread from D to E a second time and pull taut to form the next backstitch.

6 Repeat the stitch sequence across the row.

7 Turn the work 180°. Stitch the second row as a mirror image to the first.

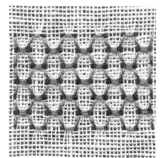

8 Continue working rows across the fabric in the same manner to fill the shape.

WAFFLE FILLING

Worked in a similar manner to honeycomb filling, waffle filling omits the horizontal backstitches, resulting in a flowing, wave-like texture. The tension of the pulled stitching causes the vertical stitches to lie on the diagonal. Each stitch is worked over four fabric threads.

1 Beginning at the right-hand side, emerge at A. Take the needle from B to C.

2 Pull the thread taut. Take the needle from D to E.

3 Pull the thread taut. Take the needle from F to G.

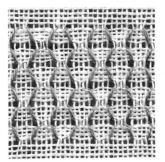

4 Pull the thread taut. Repeat the stitch sequence across the row.

5 Turn the work 180°. Stitch the second row as a mirror image to the first.

6 Continue working rows across the fabric in the same manner to fill the shape.

Bianca

PATRICIA GIROLAMI

Perfect stitches and precise cutting combine
to create this elegant Hardanger mat.
Worked onto pure white evenweave cotton
fabric with two weights of lustrous perlé
thread, the stylish design features extensive
use of needleweaving and satin stitch.
An intricate Maltese cross design surrounds
the central motif and a delicate lacy edging
borders the square.

BEFORE YOU BEGIN

Read the complete instructions

See the pullout pattern for the embroidery chart

All embroidery is worked with ONE strand of thread

THIS DESIGN USES

Blanket stitch / Diagonal cable stitch
Kloster blocks / Leviathan stitch
Madeira star stitch / Maltese cross filling
Needlewoven bar / Satin stitch
Square eyelets / Whipping

The finished mat measures 38cm (15in) square

REQUIREMENTS

Fabric

60cm (23⅝in) square of white Zweigart Brittney (Lugana) 29-count white cotton evenweave

Supplies

Light-coloured machine sewing thread

Sharp, fine pointed embroidery scissors

43cm (17in) square embroidery frame

Needles

No. 22 tapestry
No. 24 tapestry

Threads

DMC no. 8 perlé cotton
A = blanc
DMC no. 12 perlé cotton
B = blanc

PREPARATION FOR EMBROIDERY

PREPARING THE FABRIC

Machine stitch or overlock the raw edges of the fabric to prevent it from fraying.

Fold the fabric in half along the straight grain to find the approximate centre. Using the light-coloured machine sewing thread tack along the fold following a fabric thread, tacking over four and under four threads.

Fold the fabric in half again in the opposite direction. Starting at the centre and leaving a long tail, tack over four and under four threads, beginning two threads from the centre of the first row.

Rethread the tail into the needle and complete the second half (diag 1).

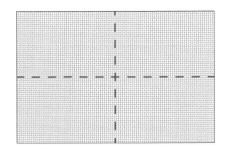

EMBROIDERY

See pages 33–34 and 36–37 for step-by-step instructions for working diagonal cable stitch, needlewoven bars, leviathan stitch, kloster blocks, Maltese cross filling and part Maltese cross/wrapping/blanket stitch.

Refer to the embroidery chart and close-up photograph for stitch placement.

The no. 22 tapestry needle is used when working with the no. 8 perlé cotton and the no. 24 is used when working with the no. 12 perlé cotton.

ORDER OF WORK

Start with a waste knot to secure the thread on the surface, about 7cm (2¾in) to the side of the first stitch. To end off, take the needle and thread to the back and slide the needle through the completed stitches, working one or two small backstitches.

CENTRE SQUARE

Referring to the embroidery chart for placement and using **A**, work the kloster blocks that outline the centre square, starting at the right-hand block working upwards and following the step-by-step instructions. Work a second row next to the first to complete the innermost border.

Using **B**, stitch the square eyelets at the centre of each group of four kloster blocks following the step-by-step instructions.

Following the chart, work the second row of kloster blocks and square eyelets in the same manner.

> HINTS
>
> *"When working the kloster blocks you will need to keep checking that the blocks are lined up correctly. To help with this I recommend that you work tacking stitches as guidelines across the fabric, working over and under four threads corresponding with the centre lines. Work in bands of 24 to 40 threads, depending upon the design. These grid lines will help you to line up the kloster blocks on the opposite side. This may seem a chore but it could save a whole lot of heartache later if the blocks don't match up."* **PATRICIA**
>
> *Using light-coloured machine sewing thread ensures that any fibres left in the fabric when the tacking has been removed will not be visible.*

STAR AND LOZENGE BORDER

Referring to the embroidery chart for placement and using **A**, work the border. Following the step-by-step instructions and using **B**, embroider a leviathan stitch at the centre of each corner star. Work the Madeira star stitch at the centre of each lozenge shape using the same thread (diag 2).

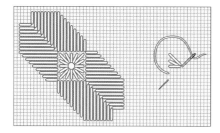

CLOVER AND CABLE STITCH BORDER

Using **A**, work the inner satin stitch four leaf clover border (diag 3).

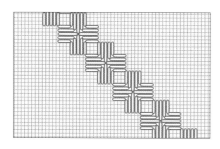

Using **B**, stitch the border of diagonal double cable stitch (diag 4).

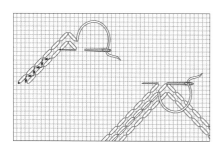

Using **A**, work the outer satin stitch four leaf clover border in the same manner as before.

CENTRE SQUARE

Cut and withdraw the required threads from the large central section, removing four threads from each alternate pair of kloster blocks.

Following the step-by-step instructions and using **B**, work the needlewoven bars over groups of four threads, carrying the working thread across the back of the work between the bars (diag 5).

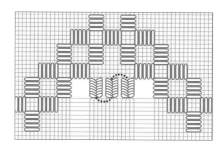

INNER BORDER

Following the chart in the pullout pattern, cut and withdraw the threads from the band between the two rows of kloster blocks.

Using **B**, work the Maltese cross filling between the two rows of kloster blocks, following the step-by-step instructions.

OUTER LACE BORDER

On the outer edge of the outer four leaf clover border, cut and withdraw threads from the end of each satin stitch block, leaving a grid of four by four threads eight blocks deep (diag 6).

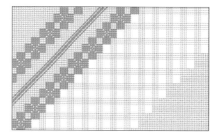

Referring to the embroidery chart for placement and the step-by-step instructions and using **A**, work needlewoven bars over groups of four threads, forming a square mesh.

Carefully following the embroidery chart and using **B**, work a row of part Maltese cross filling over the next two threads around the edge following the step-by-step instructions.

Using **B**, work a row of whipped bars over the remaining two threads in the group with blanket stitch corners at each thread intersection (diag 7).

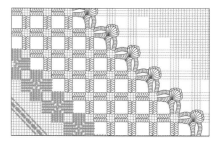

Repeat the previous two rows.

SCALLOPED EDGE

Following the embroidery chart for stitch placement, work the outer edge in woven bars and blanket stitch using **A** (diag 8).

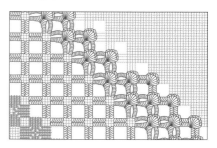

Cut away the excess fabric close to the edge of the stitches.

Place the embroidery face down onto a well-padded surface and press gently.

DIAGONAL CABLE STITCH

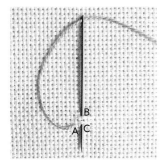

1 **First row.** Bring the thread to the front at A. Take the thread to the back at B and emerge at C.

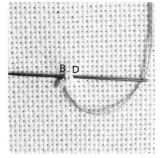

2 Take the thread to the back at D and re-emerge at B.

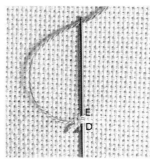

3 Take the thread to the back at E and re-emerge at D.

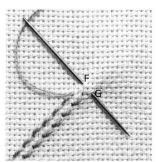

4 Continue working in this manner to the corner. Take the needle to the back at F and emerge at G.

5 Take the needle to the back at F again and emerge at H.

6 Take the needle to the back at I and re-emerge at G. Repeat steps 3–6.

7 **Second row.** Bring the thread to the front at J. Take it to the back at K and emerge at L.

8 Take the needle to the back at M. Emerge at N. Work a second row of stitches inside the first.

9 Continue working the second row of cable stitch as before.

NEEDLEWOVEN BARS

Needlewoven bars are used to create the lace border and in groups of three to form the mesh in the centre square.

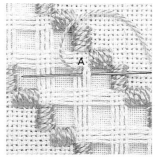

1 Bring the thread to the front at A. Take the needle around two threads and re-emerge at A.

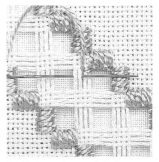

2 Tighten the stitch. Take the needle around the two threads on the left and come up through the centre.

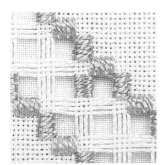

3 Tighten the stitch. Continue in this manner until the bar is filled with six stitches on each side.

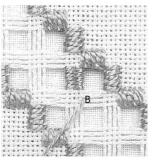

4 Carry the thread behind the fabric and bring to the front at B to begin the next bar.

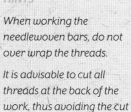

HINTS

When working the needlewoven bars, do not over wrap the threads.

It is advisable to cut all threads at the back of the work, thus avoiding the cut threads being visible on the right side.

LEVIATHAN STITCH

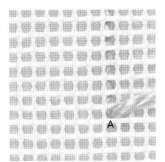

1 Secure the thread. Bring it to the front at A, on the upper left-hand side. This is the lower right-hand corner of the stitch.

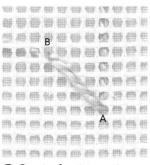

2 Crossing four intersections, take needle to back at B. This is the upper left-hand corner of the stitch. Pull the thread through.

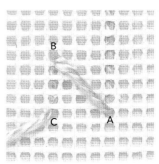

3 Emerge at C, four threads below B. Pull the thread through.

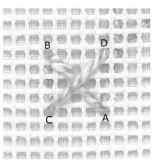

4 Crossing four intersections, take the needle to the back at D in the upper right-hand corner of the stitch. Pull the thread through.

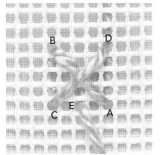

5 Emerge at E, halfway between A and C. Pull the thread through.

6 Crossing four threads, take the needle to the back at F, directly above. Pull the thread through.

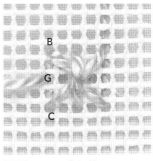

7 Emerge at G, halfway between B and C. Pull the thread through.

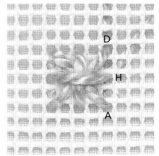

8 Crossing four threads to the right, take the needle to the back at H. Pull the thread through.

KLOSTER BLOCKS

Kloster blocks consist of five parallel stitches over a grid of four by four fabric threads. Each block is worked at a right angle to the previous one.

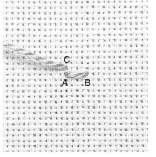

1 Bring the thread to the front at A. Take it to the back at B and bring it to the front at C.

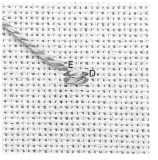

2 Take the thread to the back at D and bring it to the front at E.

3 Continue until five stitches have been worked.

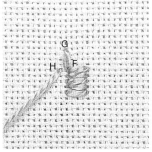

4 Bring the thread to the front at F and take it to the back at G. Emerge at H.

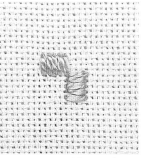

5 Continue until five stitches have been worked.

MALTESE CROSS FILLING

Commonly known as Greek cross filling, this stitch is worked over an intersection of four by four threads. Work one quarter at a time, taking note of the number of wraps.

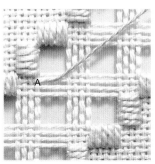

1 Bring the thread to the front at A.

2 Tightly wrap a pair of threads to B.

3 Bring the thread to the front at C. Take it back over the thread pair and under the wrapped threads.

4 Take the thread over the wrapped threads and under the unwrapped threads.

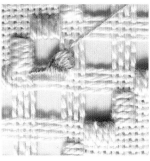

5 Continue working in a figure 8, easing the stitch tension to create a fan shape.

6 Wrap the remaining pair of threads back to the kloster block edge.

7 Repeat steps 1 to 4.

8 Repeat steps 5 and 6.

9 Repeat this sequence of stitching twice more to complete the Maltese cross.

PART MALTESE CROSS / WRAPPING / BLANKET STITCH

We outlined the cut threads with kloster blocks to hold the cut fabric threads in place.

1 Work one quarter of Maltese cross filling in the same manner as before. Bring the needle to the front at A.

2 Tightly wrap the pair of threads to the thread intersection.

3 Take the needle from B to C, ensuring that the thread is under the needle tip.

4 Take the needle from B to D, again ensuring that the thread is under the needle tip.

5 Continue working blanket stitch over the thread intersection and between each thread, always taking the needle to the back at B.

6 Slide the needle under the remaining pair of threads.

7 Wrap the threads back to the intersection.

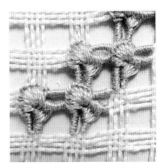

8 Complete the row. Work a second row, offsetting it to the first, as shown.

Tulip

CHRISTINE P. BISHOP

*Perfect in design and execution, this
exquisite white linen sachet features an
elegant, single tulip motif filled with
delicate Hedebo needlelace and finished
with eyelets and satin stitch.*

*The upper edge of the sachet features
sawtooth shaping interspersed with ornate
needlelace motifs and dainty cutwork
domes. Edged along the sides and base with
Hedebo stitch, the sachet contains a pink
silk pillow filled with lavender and is tied
with a wide, white grosgrain ribbon.*

REQUIREMENTS

Fabric

20 x 50cm wide (8 x 20in) piece of white handkerchief linen

14 x 30cm wide (5½ x 12in) piece of rose silk dupion

Supplies

1m x 22mm wide (40 x ⅞in) white grosgrain ribbon

Sewing thread to match silk

15cm (6in) embroidery hoop

3.25mm (no. 10) knitting needle or couronne stick

Dressmaker's awl

Pins

10 x 25cm wide (4 x 10in) piece of light-coloured card

10 x 25cm wide (4 x 10in) piece of adhesive film

Dried lavender

Tracing paper

Fine black pen

Sharp 2H pencil

Needles

No. 9 crewel

No. 24 tapestry

Thread

DMC no. 80 dentelles
B5200 snow white (5g ball)

DMC stranded cotton
B5200 snow white

BEFORE YOU BEGIN

Read the complete instructions and pullout pattern

See the pullout pattern for the embroidery design, templates and pattern

All embroidery is worked with ONE strand of thread

THIS DESIGN USES

Buttonhole stitch / Eyelet
Hedebo picot stitch / Hedebo stitch
Padded satin stitch / Running stitch
Whipping

The finished sachet measures
23 x 15cm wide (9 x 6in)

PREPARATION FOR EMBROIDERY

PREPARING THE FABRIC

Cut the linen in half so that each piece measures 20 x 25cm wide (8 x 10in). Neaten the edges of the linen with a machine zigzag or overlock stitch to prevent fraying.

TRANSFERRING THE DESIGN

Trace the pattern, placement marks and embroidery design onto the tracing paper with the black pen. Using a lightbox or window if necessary, centre one linen piece over the tracing, aligning the straight grain with the placement marks, and tape in place. Transfer the pattern and design using the pencil. Repeat for the second linen piece, omitting the tulip design. This will be the sachet back.

PREPARING THE TEMPLATES

Using the black pen, trace the templates for the needlelace edge and centre petal filling onto tracing paper and cut out. Tape to the card, leaving enough space to cut around each template, and cover with the adhesive film. Cut out each template. For the petal filling template, cut along the short lines marked around the outer edge.

EMBROIDERY

See pages 50–51 for step-by-step instructions for working Hedebo stitch and eyelets.

The stranded cotton is used for the eyelets and padded satin stitch. The dentelles thread is used for all other embroidery. Use the tapestry needle for the needlelace and the crewel needle for all surface embroidery. Hedebo embroidery is usually worked in the hand, however the tulip motif should be worked in the hoop.

ORDER OF WORK

Omitting the eyelets and small teardrop shapes, outline the cut work shapes and sachet pattern with running stitch on both linen pieces, working on the design line and using the dentelles. Once all outlines are complete, press the work before commencing the embroidery. Every shape will be outlined with a second row of running stitch and this second row is stitched as you are about to work on each shape.

---

1 | SMALL DOMES

There are two small dome shapes along the upper edge of each sachet piece. Cut the fabric and complete the embroidery on one shape at a time.

Cut a 70cm (28in) length of the dentelles. Beginning at A, edge the shape with the second row of running stitch just outside the first. Leave the thread aside at A. If you are left handed, begin from the opposite side. Using sharp embroidery scissors, cut the fabric inside the shape following the diagram (diag 1).

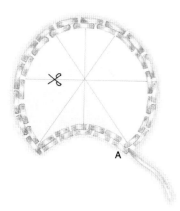

Finger press the cut fabric to the back at the first line of running stitch.

● DOME FILLING

1 | Foundation. Beginning at A with the same thread from the running stitch, work a foundation row of 30 Hedebo stitches around the shape keeping the stitches 2mm (¹⁄₁₆in) apart. Link the first and last stitches.

2 | On the wrong side, carefully trim away the excess fabric flaps to the edge of the stitching.

3 | Open Hedebo stitch. Work around the dome from A to B, making one Hedebo stitch into every second foundation stitch. Take care not to pull the loops too tight as you work. At B, anchor the thread through the fabric.

4 | Whip the loops from B back around the curve to A. Take the thread through the fabric at A and under the stitching on the wrong side. Emerge at B.

5 | Arches. Throw the thread to C, taking the thread through the fabric, then back to B, taking the thread through the loop.

6 | Work Hedebo stitch over the arch from B to C. Anchor the thread through the fabric.

7 | Throw the thread to A, then back to C. Work Hedebo stitch from C to D, halfway along the arch.

8 | Throw the thread to E, halfway along the previous arch, to D and back to E.

9 | Work Hedebo stitch from E to D, and then to A. Secure the thread under the stitching on the wrong side.

DOME FILLING

NOTES

Open Hedebo stitch is Hedebo stitch worked across a larger space and not pulled firmly.

To 'throw' a thread

A thread is taken back and forth between two points to make the foundation for a bar or arch, and is anchored under a loop or through the fabric at that point.

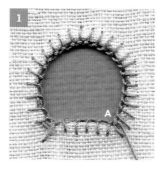

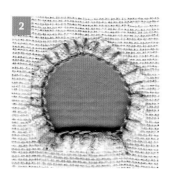

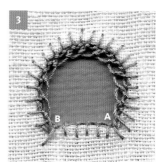

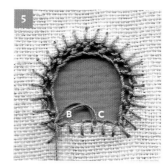

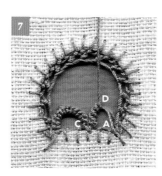

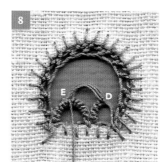

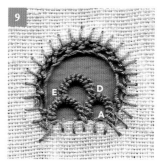

2 | EYELETS

Using a single strand of stranded cotton, work the eyelets beneath the domes and surrounding the centre petal of the tulip motif following the instructions on page 51.

3 | TULIP OUTER PETALS

Beginning with the right-hand petal, rotate the work so that the petal is aligned horizontally with the outermost edge of the petal at the lower edge. Mount the work in the hoop and edge the shape with the second row of running stitch, just outside the first. Cut the fabric as indicated (diag 2).

Finger press the cut fabric to the back at the first running stitch line. Embroider Hedebo stitch around the shape, beginning at either of the pointed ends.

● LOOPS, BARS AND POINTS

Referring to the close-up photograph, determine the spacing of the loops along the lower edge. You may find it helpful to mark a dot at each position using a heat-soluble marker.

1 | Loops. Run the thread behind the stitches along the edge and emerge at A. Work a buttonhole stitch to secure the thread (diag 3).

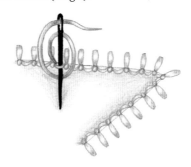

2 | Throw the thread to B and back to A, anchoring through a loop.

3 | Work reverse Hedebo stitch from A to B.

4 | Run the thread under the edge stitching to C. Secure the thread through the fabric edge with a buttonhole stitch.

5 | Throw the thread from C to D and work reverse Hedebo stitch back to C.

6 | In the same manner, work a further 14 evenly spaced loops along the edge.

7 | For the final loop, run the thread under the edge stitching around the point to E. Throw the thread to the previous loop and work reverse Hedebo stitch back to E.

8 | Open Hedebo stitch. Work a row of open Hedebo stitch across the top of the loops, placing two stitches across each loop. Whip back to the left-hand side and anchor the thread through the fabric.

NOTE *Reverse Hedebo stitch is Hedebo stitch worked from right to left.*

LOOPS

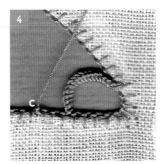

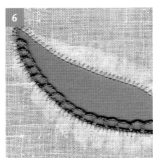

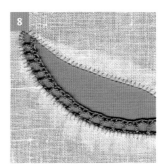

● BARS AND POINTS

Referring to the close-up photograph as a guide, determine the spacing along the row of open Hedebo stitches and the opposite edge of the petal for the wrapped bars and Hedebo points that are worked along the shape. The points have a base of seven stitches. You may find it helpful to mark the positions of the bars and points with a dot using a heat-soluble marker.

9 | Bar. Whip along the open Hedebo stitches to the position for the first wrapped bar. Throw the thread from the loop to the fabric edge, back to the loop and back to the fabric edge. If necessary, begin a new thread at this point.

10 | Wrap the bar back to the loop and whip to the position for the first Hedebo point.

11 | Hedebo point. Work the seven base stitches, placing two or three stitches per open Hedebo stitch as needed on your piece.

12 | Whip back over the base stitches.

13 | Missing the first stitch, work Hedebo stitches to the end of the base row.

14 | Whip back over the stitches.

15 | Continue working decreasing rows of stitches until you complete the Hedebo point with a row containing a single stitch.

16 | Throw the thread across to a loop on the opposite edge, referring to your previously determined spacing, taking the thread through the loop from top to bottom. Pull the thread through.

17 | Throw back to the tip of the Hedebo point, then back to the edge loop. Wrap the thread back to the Hedebo point and whip down the right-hand side to the base.

To complete the right hand petal, work four more Hedebo points and a second wrapped bar, whipping along the open Hedebo stitches between each.

Prepare the left hand petal in the same manner as the right-hand petal. Beginning at the left-hand end, work 17 loops along the outer edge in a similar manner as before. For the loops on this petal, the Hedebo stitches are worked from left to right. Work a row of open Hedebo stitches across the loops as for the previous petal. Complete the petal filling with two wrapped bars and five Hedebo points worked along the row of open Hedebo stitches.

BARS AND POINTS

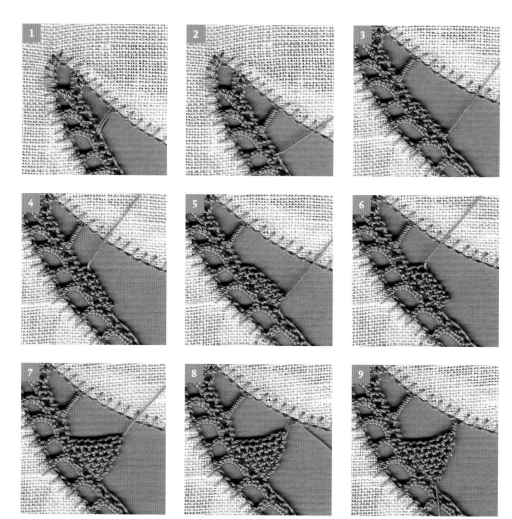

4 | TULIP CENTRE PETAL

Beginning at the tip, edge the shape with the second row of running stitch just outside the first and cut the fabric as shown (diag 4).

Finger press the cut fabric to the back at the first running stitch line.

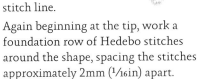

Again beginning at the tip, work a foundation row of Hedebo stitches around the shape, spacing the stitches approximately 2mm (¹⁄₁₆in) apart.

● FLOWER

To work the elements of the small flower, you will need the prepared centre petal template and the 3.25mm (no. 10) knitting needle or 3mm diameter section of a couronne stick.

1 | **Small petals.** Cut a 60cm (24in) length of dentelles and wrap one end around the knitting needle three times and secure with a buttonhole stitch. Remove from the needle and work Hedebo stitch around the ring, covering all of the threads. Link the last stitch with the first.

2 | Continuing in the same direction, make a Hedebo point with three base stitches. At the tip of the point, work another Hedebo stitch back into the last stitch, from right to left.

3 | Using the sewing thread, tack the small petal over a corresponding shape on the template, with the point outermost. Leave the thread tail aside, placing it through the nearest slot around the outer edge of the template.

4 | Make a further six small petals, and tack to the template.

5 | **Centre.** Cut a 60cm (24in) length of dentelles and wrap one end around the knitting needle three

times and secure with a buttonhole stitch. Remove from the needle and position on the template, ensuring the buttonhole stitch aligns with one of the lines connecting to a petal. Tack the ring in place with seven tiny stitches, evenly spaced around the ring.

6 | Work four Hedebo stitches over the ring. Throw the thread to the edge of the nearest small petal and whip back to the centre ring, anchoring the thread through the last Hedebo stitch.

7 | Repeat this sequence until ready to connect the seventh petal. For the final petal, throw the thread from the centre to the edge of the petal and back to the centre. Whip back to the petal.

FLOWER

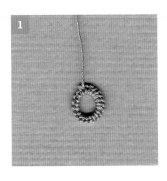

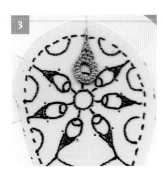

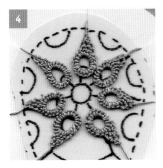

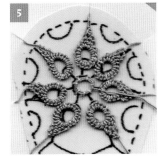

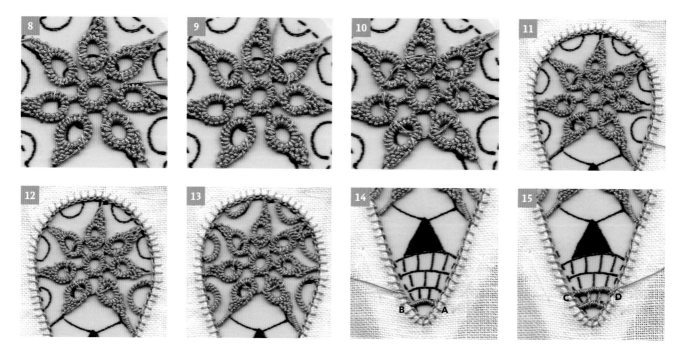

8 | Linking circle. Continue to whip around the edge of the petal to the point indicated on the template (A).

9 | Take the thread to the adjacent petal. Go up through a stitch on the first edge at the point marked on the template, across the centre and down through a stitch on the second edge. Do not go through the template.

10 | Continue around the flower, linking the petals in this manner.

When you reach the beginning, whip the circle in the same direction. Work the whipping so that the thread passes over the linking circle thread and under each petal edge as you move around the circle. Whip along the edge of a small petal, including the Hedebo point, to secure this thread. Trim away the excess.

Attaching the flower filling

Pin the template beneath the prepared centre petal on the linen. Attach one

small petal of the filling at a time, using the reserved thread tails.

11 | Remove the thread tail from the template, throw to the fabric edge and back to the small petal tip. Whip back to the fabric edge. Run the thread under the Hedebo stitches, to the position for the adjacent arch.

12 | Throw the thread across and back to form the foundation for the arch, and work Hedebo stitch over the looped threads. To end off, run the thread under the Hedebo stitches along the edge of the shape.

13 | Work the remaining petals and arches in the same manner. To finish, secure the thread under the Hedebo stitches after wrapping the bar.

● BARS

Referring to the template, work the bars and open Hedebo stitches at the pointed end of the petal.

14 | Secure a thread under the Hedebo stitches at A. Throw the thread across to B and back to A. Wrap the threads back to B.

15 | Take the thread under the edge to C. Work two open Hedebo stitches from C to D. Whip back to C, then wrap back to D.

46

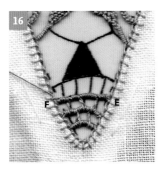
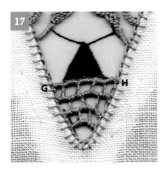
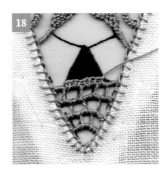
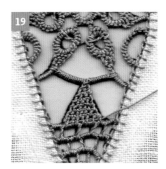

16 | Take the thread under the edge to E. Work three reverse open Hedebo stitches from E to F. Whip back to E, then wrap back to F.

17 | Take the thread under the edge to G. Work four open Hedebo stitches from G to H. Whip back to G, then wrap back to H. Secure the thread under the edge.

● **HEDEBO POINT**

18 | Begin a new thread with a waste knot at the back of the template, and emerge at the right-hand side of the

position for the Hedebo point. Take the thread across and secure on the bar at the left-hand side of the base of the point with a buttonhole stitch. Work the Hedebo point using a base row of seven or eight stitches, enclosing the wrapped bar and thread tail.

19 | When reaching the tip, throw the thread over the centre of the bar to the right-hand side that connects the lower small petal to the edge of the fabric. Return to the tip. Throw the thread over the centre of the bar to the left and return to the tip.

Throw the thread again over the bar to the right and wrap back to the point. Repeat for the left-hand side. Whip down the right-hand side of the point and finish off the thread under the base row.

Trim away the thread tail. Remove the template, taking care to only clip the tacking threads and the knots. On the wrong side of the fabric carefully trim away the excess fabric to the edge of the stitching around the petals.

---

5 | PADDED SATIN STITCH

Embroider each shape separately – do not carry the thread from one shape to the next. Using a single strand of stranded cotton, work a layer of straight stitches along the length of the shape for padding. Cover the padding with satin stitch worked at a right-angle to the straight stitches.

---

6 | NEEDLELACE EDGE

Embroider the needlelace edge for each sachet piece in the same manner. To prepare each piece, stitch the second row of running stitch around the entire outer edge. Cut out, leaving a seam allowance of 5mm (³/₁₆in). Snip into the valleys along the upper edge and fold the seam allowance under to the running stitch and finger press. For the peaks along the upper edge, first fold under the left-hand side and

then the right-hand side. Embroider Hedebo stitch around the entire outer edge, making sure that there is a loop at the very tip of each peak (diag 5).

On the wrong side carefully trim away the excess fabric to the edge of the stitching.

Tack the upper edge of one piece to the prepared needlelace template, aligning the edge of the fabric with the corresponding lines on the template. Complete the needlelace edge before removing the template. Repeat for the second piece.

● **MAIN MOTIF**

Refer to the template for placement throughout.

Bars

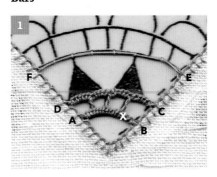

1 | Cut an 80cm (32in) length of dentelles. Using a waste knot bring the thread through the template at 'X'. Throw the thread to A, to B and back to A. Work Hedebo stitch from A to B, enclosing the thread tail.

Run the thread under the stitching along the edge to C. Embroider three large, open Hedebo stitches from C to D. Whip back to C and whip again back to D. Using sewing thread, couch these stitches to the template in three places to hold each of the loops in place. Work Hedebo stitch from D to C.

Take the thread under the edge stitching from C to E. Throw the thread to F and back to E.

Leave the thread in reserve. Using sewing thread, couch the bar between E and F to the template with six stitches, ensuring that there is a couching stitch at the position that each Hedebo point will connect with the bar. Secure the couching thread on the back of the template.

Hedebo points

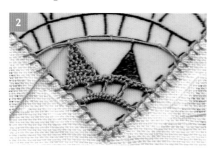

2 | Begin with a new, long thread. Knot the tail and emerge through the template at the right-hand side of the first Hedebo point. Take the thread across to the left-hand side and work a base row of six to seven Hedebo stitches, enclosing the thread tail. Complete the Hedebo point.

Throw the thread over the bar above at the indicated point, taking the thread through the couching stitch.

3 | Whip the thread once, then whip down the right-hand side of the pyramid. Continuing with the same thread, work the second Hedebo point. After whipping down the right-hand side of the pyramid, whip to the fabric edge and end off the thread under the stitching.

Upper bars

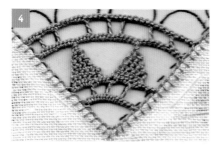

4 | Begin with a new, long thread. Knot the tail and emerge through the template near the tip of the first Hedebo point. Take the thread through the edge of the fabric at F and work Hedebo stitch to E, enclosing the thread tail.

Take the thread under the edge to G. Work seven large, reverse open Hedebo stitches from G to H. Whip back to G, then whip again back to H. Using sewing thread, couch the bar between G and H to the template ensuring that there is a couching stitch worked at the position for each vertical bar. Embroider Hedebo stitch back to G and leave any remaining thread in reserve at this point.

Arches

Refer to the template for placement and the diagram for the stitching path. The arches are worked back and forth in a diagonal pattern, beginning with the lower left arch. After forming the foundation of an arch with thrown threads, place a pin in the template at the centre of the arch to hold the threads in shape (pins not shown).

5 | Using a new thread, knot the tail and emerge through the template at the right-hand side of the first arch. To form the foundation, throw the thread through the fabric edge to the left, through the Hedebo stitch on the bar at the right-hand side of the arch, and back to the fabric edge.

Place a pin and cover the threads with Hedebo stitch from left to right.

6 | Whip along the bar to the start of the next arch. Form the foundation by throwing the thread to the right and back to the left. Work Hedebo stitch to the point where the arch above connects.

7 | Form the foundation for the connecting arch by throwing the thread back to the point indicated on the first arch, back to the second arch, and back to the first arch. Place a pin and work Hedebo stitch along the arch to the marked point for a picot.

Hedebo picot

8 | Take the thread under the bar, leaving a loop.

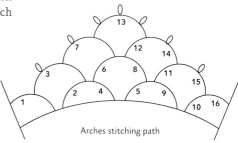

Arches stitching path

MAIN MOTIF

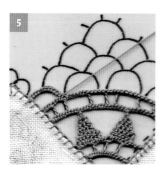

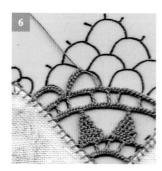

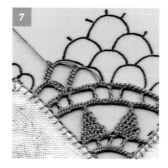

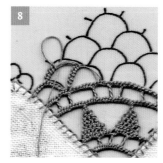

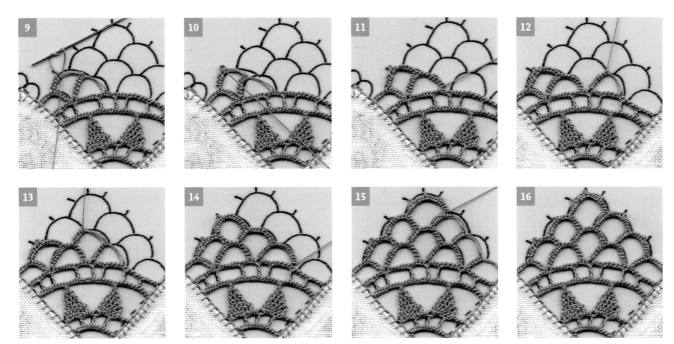

9 | Place the needle through the loop and around the thread as shown, so that the thread is twisted twice around the needle.

10 | Pull the needle and thread through. Take the needle back through the base of the stitch to complete the picot and tighten the thread.

11 | Complete the arch with Hedebo stitch and continue the Hedebo stitch along section four of the diagram.

12 | Whip along the bar and throw the thread across and back to form the foundation for the next arch. Place a pin and work Hedebo stitch to the start of the next connecting arch (section five).

13 | Throw the thread to the left, right and left to form the foundation for the connecting arch. Place a pin and work Hedebo stitch along section six, to the start of the next arch above.

14 | Throw the thread in the same manner as before to form the arch foundation. Work Hedebo stitch along section seven, working a

Hedebo picot at the marked point. Continue working Hedebo stitch down to the arch below, along section eight, and down to the arch below, along section nine.

15 | Whip along to the last arch in the bottom row. To form the foundation, throw the thread to the fabric edge at the right and back. Work section ten with Hedebo stitch. Throw the thread for the arch above, left-right-left, and work section eleven with Hedebo stitch. Throw the thread for the arch above and work section twelve with Hedebo stitch. Throw the thread for the arch above and work Hedebo stitch along the uppermost arch, adding Hedebo picots as indicated.

16 | Continue the Hedebo stitch down to complete the arches below, covering sections fourteen, fifteen and sixteen, adding picots at the marked points.

Secure the thread under the edge stitching. Remove the pins. Complete the remaining two sections in the same manner.

Beginning a new thread

If you need to bring in a new thread before the arches are complete, it is best to do so along the lower row of arches. Leave a tail of the old thread along the path of an arch and lay in the new thread back along the same path. If possible, bring in the new thread from a fabric edge and whip along to the arch you are working. Take the thread to the required position and recommence working Hedebo stitch, enclosing the old and new thread tails. Trim the old thread tail close to the stitching at the base of an arch, or take to the fabric edge to finish off.

● PEAK

Using any of the reserved threads, embroider the three arches at the peaks along the upper edge of the sachet pieces in a similar manner to the three arches within the small dome motifs.

End off any remaining thread tails from reserved threads under the stitching along the fabric edge.

MAKING THE SACHET

Wash the sachet pieces carefully in warm water using a pure soap or detergent. Rinse thoroughly in distilled water and roll the linen in a towel to remove excess moisture. Place the work face down on a soft, padded surface and press dry, protecting the linen with a pressing cloth such as a white handkerchief.

Place the front and back sachet pieces with wrong sides together, aligning edges and points. Using the dentelles, whip together around the side and lower edges, working through the loops of the previous stitching. Work a small arch across the joined point at each side.

CONSTRUCTING THE INSERT

See the pullout pattern.

HEDEBO STITCH

Also known as Hedebo buttonhole and Danish buttonhole, this knotted stitch is characteristic of Hedebo embroidery and is used to edge cut shapes.

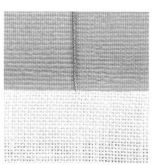

1 Secure the thread and bring it to the surface at the folded edge of the fabric.

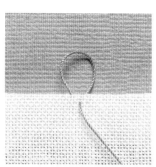

2 Take a stitch through the fabric and pull through leaving a small loop.

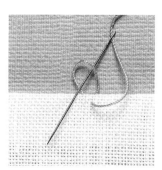

3 Take the needle through the loop, from back to front.

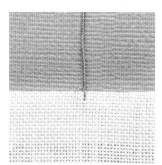

4 Pull the thread up until the knot tightens and the loop sits firmly.

5 Make a second stitch and pull the thread through leaving a small loop.

6 Take the needle through the loop, from back to front and pull the thread up as before.

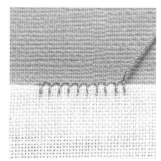

7 Continue working in this manner around the shape.

EYELETS

Eyelets are used in a variety of styles of whitework embroidery and beautifully enhance Christine's Hedebo design. They are best worked with an awl or stiletto but a large needle will suffice.

1 Mark a tiny circle on the fabric. Leaving a short tail, work a row of running stitches around the marked circle, leaving tiny stitches at the back.

2 Work a split stitch through the first stitch in the circle, then bring the thread to the front just outside the outline at A.

3 Trim the tail close to the fabric. Using an awl, piece the fabric and open up the eyelet.

4 Take the needle down through the hole and emerge on the outer edge. Pull the thread firmly.

5 Continue working overcast stitches until two stitches from completing the circle. Work the final two stitches leaving them loose.

6 Take needle back through the two stitches and pull the thread until the loops sit firmly on the fabric. Snip the thread close to the stitching.

7 Using the awl, re-pierce the eyelet from the front and back. This helps to settle the thread and fabric.

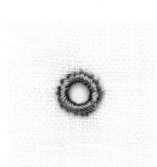

Finished eyelet.

Vintage

JUDY STEPHENSON

*The form and texture of the raised
embroidery is perfectly framed by the
counted stitchwork of the border, decorative
side seams and edging. Twisted cords are
held by neat blanket stitch loops and are
finished with beautifully decorated tassels.
The traditional monochromatic colour
scheme of the chosen fabric and threads
serves to concentrate the eye on the beauty
and form of the embroidery.*

BEFORE YOU BEGIN

*Read the complete instructions
and pullout pattern*

*See the pullout pattern for the
embroidery design*

*All embroidery is worked with ONE
strand of thread unless specified*

THIS DESIGN USES

Backstitch / Blanket stitch / Buttonhole edging
Couching / Detached blanket stitch
Double detached blanket stitch / Four-sided stitch
Italian insertion stitch / Satin stitch / Stem stitch
Tassel making / Twisted cord / Wrapping

**The finished bag measures
22 x 21cm (8⅝ x 8¼in) wide**

REQUIREMENTS

Fabric

50 x 25cm wide (20 x 10in) piece of cream 25-count Laguna linen

50 x 25cm wide (20 x 10in) piece of ivory satin

Supplies

10cm (4in) square of cream wool felt

30 x 5cm wide (12 x 2in) piece of medium-weight non-woven interfacing

Contrasting sewing thread

Small amount of toy filling

20cm (8in) embroidery hoop

11 x 8mm (⁵⁄₁₆in) natural wooden beads

Tracing paper

Sharp HB pencil

Craft glue

Wooden skewer

Needles

No. 5 milliner's

No. 24 tapestry (2)

Threads

DMC stranded cotton

A = ecru (2 skeins)

B = 3033 vy lt putty groundings (2 skeins)

DMC no. 5 perlé cotton

C = ecru

DMC no. 8 perlé cotton

D = ecru

PREPARATION FOR EMBROIDERY

PREPARING THE FABRIC

When cutting the fabric to size, cut between the threads to keep the fabric square. Neaten all edges with a machine zigzag or overlock stitch. Turn each short end under 2cm (¾in) and tack firmly. Do not turn the sides under until the embroidery on the front is complete.

Fold the fabric in half across the width and work a row of tacking along the foldline with the machine thread. This line represents the lower edge of the bag.

Divide the front into quarters. Work lines of horizontal, then vertical tacking, beginning at the centre. Tack four threads under, then four threads over, to facilitate placement of the four-sided stitch (diag 1).

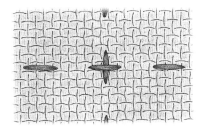

The lines of tacking remain in place until all embroidery is complete.

TRANSFERRING THE DESIGN

Using a black pen, trace the design onto the tracing paper. Tape the tracing to a window or lightbox.

With the right side up, place the prepared fabric over the tracing, aligning the tacking lines with the placement marks. Tape in place. The light shining through will make the design easy to see. Using the pencil, trace the design.

*C*asalguidi embroidery appears to have its origins in the late nineteenth century in a small village in Italy bearing the same name. This style of embroidery is a form of whitework, traditionally involving fabric which has been spun or woven from flax fibres. The use of colour is now an accepted addition.

"I find this style of embroidery very exciting because it combines the discipline of counted stitchwork as evidenced in the four-sided stitch framework, with the elements of free flowing raised design demonstrated in the branch, leaf and grapes. I am indebted to Effie Mitrofanis for the history and diverse techniques contained in her book Casalguidi Style Linen Embroidery."

JUDY

EMBROIDERY

See pages 58–60 for step-by-step instructions for working four-sided stitch, a grape, raised stem stitch branch and Italian insertion stitch side seams. See the pullout pattern for the tassel.

The embroidery design is worked with the fabric in the hoop.

Use the tapestry needle when working with the perlé cottons and when working the detached blanket stitch and the stem stitch on the branch. Use the milliner's needle for all other embroidery.

ORDER OF WORK

BORDER

Work the border of the design in four-sided stitch using **D**. Begin with the longest row, two threads from the vertical centre tacked line and sixty-two threads up from the horizontal tacked line. Work one four-sided stitch over the centre block of four threads, then work sixteen on each side of the centre, making thirty-three in all. Repeat on the remaining three sides.

Begin and end the second row at the top, four blocks in from each end of the first. Work two more rows in the same manner. Repeat on the remaining three sides.

To create the raised effect, thread the tapestry needle with a 60cm (24in) length of **C** and, leaving a short tail, bring the thread to the front inside the first four sided stitch of the long row (diag 2).

Take the thread under the vertical loops of the four-sided stitch along the row. At the end of the row, take the thread to the back just inside the last stitch. Re-emerge next to the first stitch of the next side of the border (diag 3).

Continue as before, working the thread under the vertical stitches on each side. When all four sides are complete, secure the two ends of thread carefully at the back.

Run the thread under the remaining rows of four-sided stitch, securing the tails of thread at the beginning and end of each row.

VINE

Branch

Embroider the branch following the step-by-step instructions.

Leaf

Outline the leaf shape with backstitch using three strands of **B**. Work blanket stitch over the backstitch using the same thread, ensuring the stitches are not too wide or too tight. Using **D**, work detached blanket stitch to fill one section of the leaf shape (diag 4).

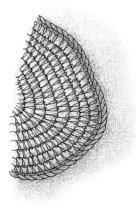

When the first section is complete, push a small amount of toy filling under the detached blanket stitch. Continue covering the leaf shape in the same manner, padding each section as you complete it.

Referring to the photograph for placement, lay down lengths of four strands of **B** for the veins. Wrap each vein with two strands of the same thread (diag 5).

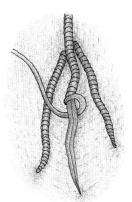

Couch in place with one strand of the same thread.

Leaf stem

Anchor four 15cm (6in) lengths of **D** on the back of the fabric at the top of the leaf for the padding. Bring the threads to the front and take them over the branch, draping them loosely, before securing on the back of the fabric (diag 6).

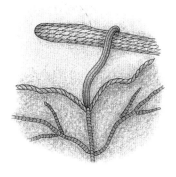

Bring four strands of **A** to the front in the same manner as the **D** threads and wrap the padding closely (diag 7).

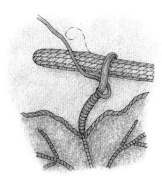

Adjust the wrapping and placement of the stem before securing the wrapping threads on the back as before.

Work a loop of four strands of **D** for padding over the branch for the next section of the stem (diag 8).

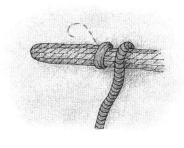

Wrap in the same manner as before using four strands of **A**. For the last section of the stem, lay the padding threads in the same manner, wrapping more tightly towards the end to give a tapered effect. Couch in place.

GRAPES

Make the eleven grapes following the step-by-step instructions, and attach them to the fabric at the marked positions.

Work the stem in the same manner as the leaf stem.

TENDRILS

The tendrils are created in the same manner as the stems, using three strands of **A** for the padding and two strands of **A** for the wrapping.

DECORATIVE SIDE SEAMS

Remove the fabric from the hoop. Turn each side of the fabric under 2cm (¾in) and tack firmly.

The strip of interfacing is used as a guide or spacer when joining the side seams with the Italian insertion stitch.

Draw two parallel lines down the centre of the interfacing, 5mm (³⁄₁₆in) apart. Work the insertion stitch following the step-by-step instructions.

LOOPS

The cord is held by five loops on the front of the bag and five on the back, all worked with **D**. Work the centre front loop first. Count up sixteen threads along the central line of tacking from the top row of four-sided stitch. Make a loop from this point over the next twelve threads by stitching twice with **D** (diag 9).

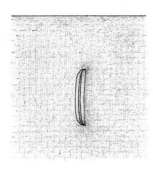

With the same thread, work double detached blanket stitch over the two

strands. Use two needles to do this, one each side of the loop, and alternate the stitches (diag 10).

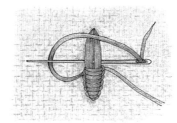

Work the next two loops 3cm (1¼in) in from the sides of the bag. The remaining two loops are evenly spaced between these three.

DECORATIVE UPPER EDGE

Use the tapestry needle to work the blanket stitch scalloped edge. Using **C** and beginning at a side seam, work a loop over the insertion stitch (diag 11).

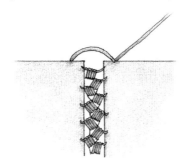

Lay the thread loosely along the top and catch the fabric nine threads further along, anchoring with a tiny stitch (diag 12).

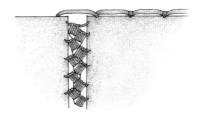

Continue in this manner until nearing the starting point. Check the number of threads remaining so that the loops can be adjusted if necessary to keep them as even as possible.

Work eight blanket stitches into each loop using the same thread. Form the scallop by taking the ninth stitch

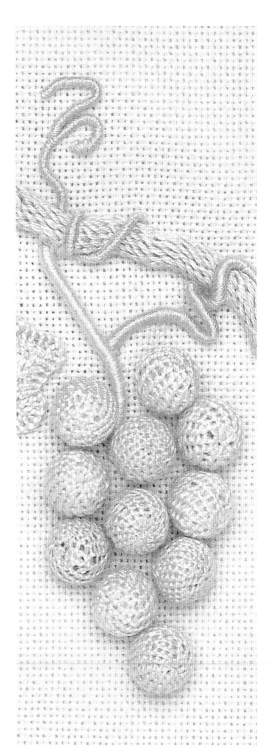

through the fabric where the loop is attached.

Change to three strands of **B** and work a second row of blanket stitch.

CORDS AND TASSELS

Make the two twisted cords and tassels following the instructions in the pullout pattern.

CONSTRUCTION

See the pullout pattern.

FOUR-SIDED STITCH

Four-sided stitch forms an attractive border for the embroidery design on the front of the bag.

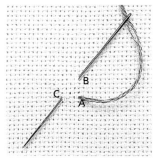

1 Bring the needle to the front at A. Take it to the back at B, four threads above A. Emerge at C, four threads below and four to the left.

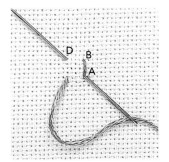

2 Pull the needle through and insert at A. Bring to the front at D, four threads above and four to the left.

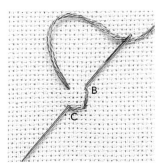

3 Insert the needle at B and re-emerge at C.

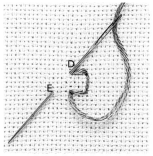

4 Insert the needle at D and emerge at E, four threads below and four to the left.

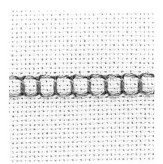

5 Continue in this manner to the end of the row.

GRAPE

*Each grape is worked with three strands of **A**, each 1m (39in) in length. It is important to have enough thread to finish the grape without having to join it.*

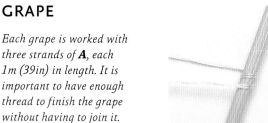

1 Wrap the threads twice around the skewer, leaving a 12cm (4¾in) tail.

2 Leaving the tail dangling, work detached blanket stitch over the threads to form a ring.

3 Put a small amount of glue on the top of a bead. Wait until it is tacky and place the ring over it.

4 Insert the pointed end of the skewer into the hole at the base of the bead.

5 Begin working detached blanket stitch into the ring, covering the tail.

6 Increase the number of stitches at the widest part of the bead and decrease as you approach the base.

7 Remove the skewer to complete the stitching at the base.

8 Thread the tail and working thread into the needle and take through the hole in the base to the top, leaving at least 10cm (4in) of each thread.

9 **Attaching the grape.** Thread both tails into the needle and attach the grape securely at the marked position.

ITALIAN INSERTION STITCH

*This decorative stitch is used to join the side seams of the bag and is worked using **D**.*

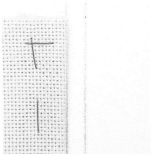

1 Place the side of the bag against one drawn line on the spacer so that the other drawn line is visible.

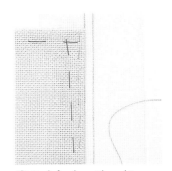

2 Tack firmly until reaching the tacking line representing the base.

3 Fold the fabric and spacer so that the top edges are even. Tack the remaining side to the second line on the spacer interfacing.

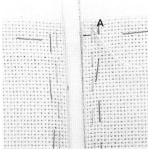

4 Italian insertion stitch. Bring the needle up at A, two threads in from the edge and two down from the top.

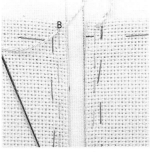

5 Take the needle from the back at B, two threads in from the edge and two down from the top.

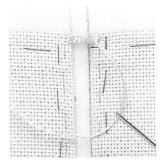

6 Repeat, working into the same holes. Work four detached blanket stitches from left to right across the loop.

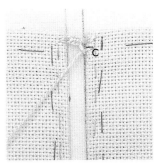

7 Work a blanket stitch on the right edge at C, two threads in from the edge and two threads down from the starting point.

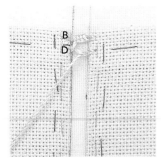

8 Work another blanket stitch on the left at D, four threads below B.

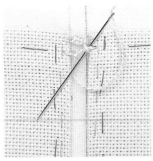

9 Work a detached blanket stitch around the centre of the blanket stitch on the right fabric edge.

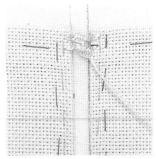

10 Work three more stitches around the same stitch, working from left to right.

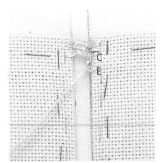

11 Work a blanket stitch on the right side at E, four threads below C.

12 Work a detached blanket stitch at the centre of the stitch on the left-hand side.

13 Work three more stitches around the same stitch, working from right to left.

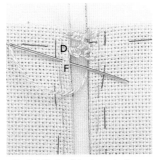

14 Work a blanket stitch on the left edge at F, four threads below D.

15 Continue in the same manner until reaching the base of the bag.

RAISED STEM STITCH BRANCH

*The raised stem stitch is worked over a layer of padding formed with ten 22cm (8½in) lengths of **D**.*
Fold the bundle in half to make twenty thicknesses. Contrasting threads have been used for clarity.

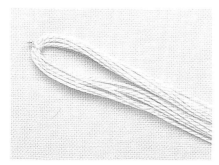

1 Secure the folded end of the threads to the top left-hand end of the marked line.

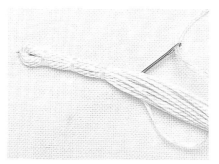

2 Using **A**, couch the padding in place. Bring the needle up on marked line, take it over padding and then back through the same hole.

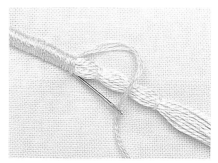

3 Using the milliner's needle and three strands of **B**, work satin stitch over the padding, angling the needle under the padding.

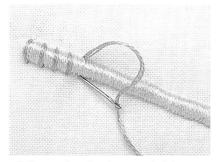

4 Create a base for the stem stitch by working a series of loose straight stitch bars at 2mm (¹⁄₁₆in) intervals using three strands of **A**.

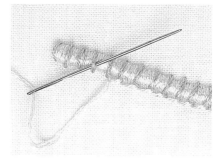

5 With three strands of **B** in the tapestry needle, work detached stem stitch over the bars, beginning at the lower right-hand end.

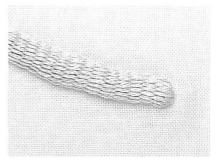

6 Begin each row at the same end, packing the rows firmly together.

A Fine
Romance

SUSAN O'CONNOR

Traditional Madeira embroidery
techniques are skilfully worked on this
delicate sachet. The elegant embroidery
is worked on a silk organdie oval, set
into white handkerchief linen. Fine pin
stitching is used to attach the oval insert
and to appliqué the leaves and petals.
Eyelets and perfectly raised granitos add
texture and dimension, while shadow
work cleverly enhances the design. The
sachet is neatly finished with a scalloped
blanket stitch edge.

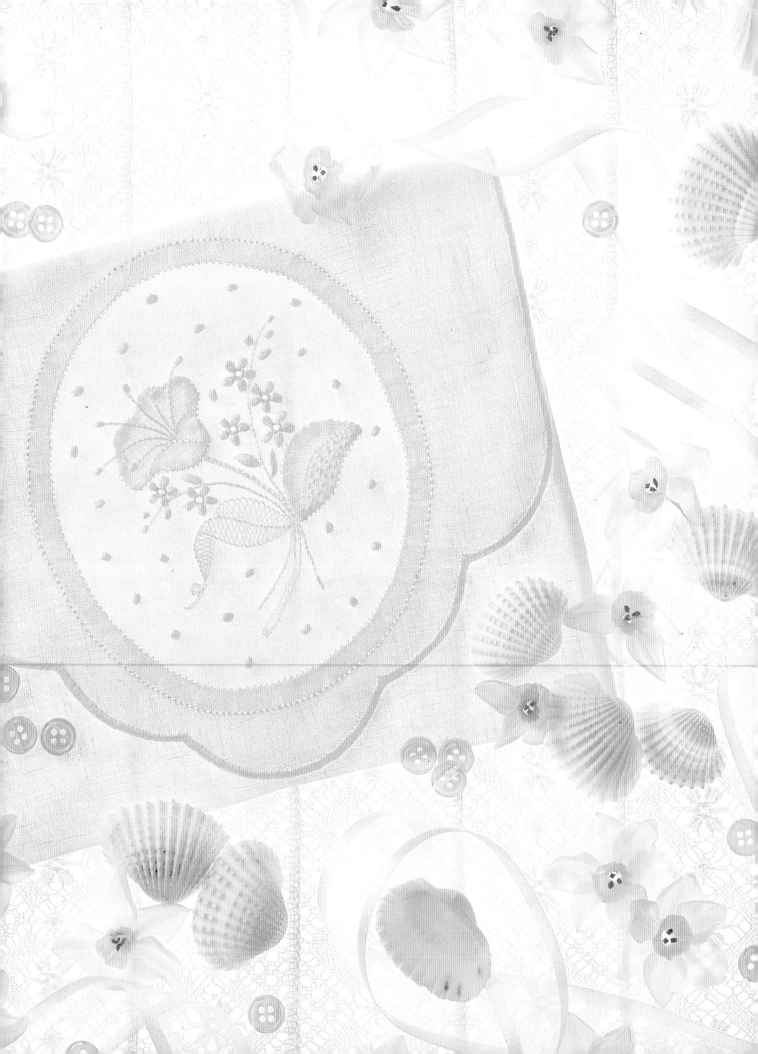

BEFORE YOU BEGIN

Read the complete instructions and pullout pattern

See the pullout pattern for the embroidery design and templates

All embroidery is worked with ONE strand of thread

THIS DESIGN USES

Backstitch / Closed herringbone stitch
Eyelet / Granitos / Padded blanket stitch
Padded satin stitch / Pin stitch
Seed stitch / Stem stitch

**The finished sachet measures
16 x 18cm wide (6¼ x 7in)**

REQUIREMENTS

Fabric

25 x 55cm wide
(10 x 21⅝in) piece of white
handkerchief linen
20cm (8in) square of white
organdie

Supplies

Dressmaker's awl
Black permanent pen
Tracing paper
Lightweight cardboard
Sharp 2H pencil

Needles

No. 7 between
No. 26 tapestry

Thread

DMC Broder Spécial no. 25
A = blanc

PREPARATION FOR EMBROIDERY

See page 69 for the step-by-step instructions for working the pin stitch.

PREPARING THE FABRICS

Cut the linen to 19.5 x 48.5cm wide (7⅞ x 19⅛in), cutting along the grain of the fabric.

Using the black pen, trace the oval templates onto tracing paper and transfer to the lightweight cardboard. Cut out and set aside.

Fold the linen in half along the length and finger press, ensuring the fold is along the straight grain of the fabric. Using a light-coloured machine sewing thread, work a row of tacking stitches along the fold line. Press and starch the linen thoroughly, applying two or three layers of starch to the fabric. The layer of starch will protect the fabric while being handled and make it easier to wash out any visible transfer markings once the project is complete. Press the organdie. Measure up 3.5cm (1⅜in) from the lower short edge on the linen along the tacked line (diag 1).

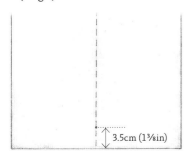

3.5cm (1⅜in)

This is the placement point for the base of the large oval. Aligning the placement marks with the row of tacking, use a very sharp pencil to lightly transfer the oval onto the linen. Carefully centre the small oval template inside the first and trace in the same manner.

Carefully cut away the inner oval of linen. Do not discard this piece as you will need it for the appliqué flower and leaf.

Using very sharp scissors, clip the linen at 1cm (⅜in) intervals to the outer marked oval and finger press to the back (diag 2).

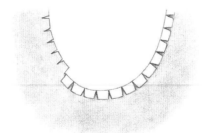

Tack in place. Carefully press the linen from the back, then the front.

The linen is cut to the exact measurements and the scalloped edge transferred after the embroidery is complete.

ATTACHING THE ORGANDIE INSERT

Centre the organdie over the oval on the wrong side of the linen. Pin and tack in place.

Using the between needle and **A**, pin stitch the fabrics together along the folded edge following the step-by-step instructions. Press.

Measure and mark a 7mm (⁵⁄₁₆in) border out from the pin stitching. This line will match the cut edges that have been folded under. Work a row of tacking 2mm (¹⁄₁₆in) inside the marked line.

Using the tapestry needle and working from the right side, pin stitch along the marked line. On the wrong side, trim away the organdie as close to the second line of pin stitching as possible. Press.

TRANSFERRING THE DESIGN

Embroidery design

Using the black pen, trace the embroidery design and placement marks onto tracing paper.

Position the oval insert over the embroidery design, aligning the tacking with the placement marks. Using the sharp pencil, trace the embroidery design. Mark the centre of each granitos spot with a dot.

Appliqué

Trace the flower and leaf templates onto the tracing paper. Place the linen oval over the tracing and pin in place. Using the pencil, transfer the designs.

Cut out the flower and leaf along the marked cutting line. Clip and finger press the seam allowance to the back. Position the flower onto the organdie and hold in place with several tacking stitches. Using the tapestry needle and **A**, work pin stitch around the flower, shaping the edges with the needle as you go. Repeat for the leaf.

EMBROIDERY

See page 69 for the step-by-step instructions for working the granitos.

The between needle is used for all remaining embroidery.

ORDER OF WORK

APPLIQUÉ FLOWER

Define the front petals with backstitch. Work the stamens in stem stitch, keeping the stitches small and ensuring each stitch shares the hole in the fabric with the previous one. Finish each stamen with a granitos. Embroider the flower stem with backstitch.

APPLIQUÉ LEAF

Stitch the vein of the leaf in back-stitch. Create shading on the right half of the leaf using seed stitch (diag 3).

SHADOW WORK LEAF

Embroider the shadow work leaf from the wrong side of the fabric, stitching each section from the base to the tip. Finish the tip of the leaf with a backstitch curl.

FLOWER SPRAYS

Work the stems in stem stitch, keeping the stitches small. Finish each stem with a tiny granitos.

The centre eyelet of each flower is worked before the petals. Leaving a tail of thread, work four straight stitches around the marked circle (diag 4).

At the last corner, sink the thread and emerge on the outer edge of the circle (diag 5).

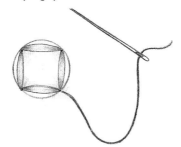

Using the awl or a large needle, make a hole in the centre of the circle (diag 6).

Take the needle down through the centre hole and emerge on the outer edge, pulling the thread firmly. Continue around the circle, working the stitches close together and pulling each one firmly (diag 7).

Stitch five granitos around each eyelet for the petals.

The leaves are worked in padded satin stitch. For the padding, stitch a figure eight in the centre of the shape (diag 8).

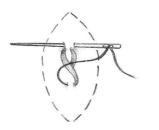

Continue until the shape is full. This form of padding creates a mound with the highest point at the centre. Work satin stitch over the padding, beginning a short distance from the point (diag 9).

Cover the remaining leaf in the same manner.

GRANITOS SPOTS

Embroider a granitos at each marked position.

SCALLOPED EDGE

Trace the scallop template onto tracing paper. Position the linen over the tracing, aligning the placement marks with the tacking and the inner edge of the oval. Trace the scalloped edge onto the linen. The edge is worked using padded blanket stitch between the marked dots. Leaving the end of the thread free at the beginning and end, work running stitches for the padding. Take smaller stitches where necessary to accommodate the curves (diag 10).

Weave the thread tails under the stitches on the back.

Work two to three rows of padding to fill the space between the two lines. To avoid puckering the fabric, do not pull too tightly.

Work close blanket stitch over the padding.

Carefully cut away the excess fabric, close to the stitches, beginning and ending with a horizontal cut at the top of the straight edge (diag 11).

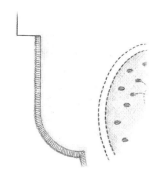

CONSTRUCTION

See the pullout pattern.

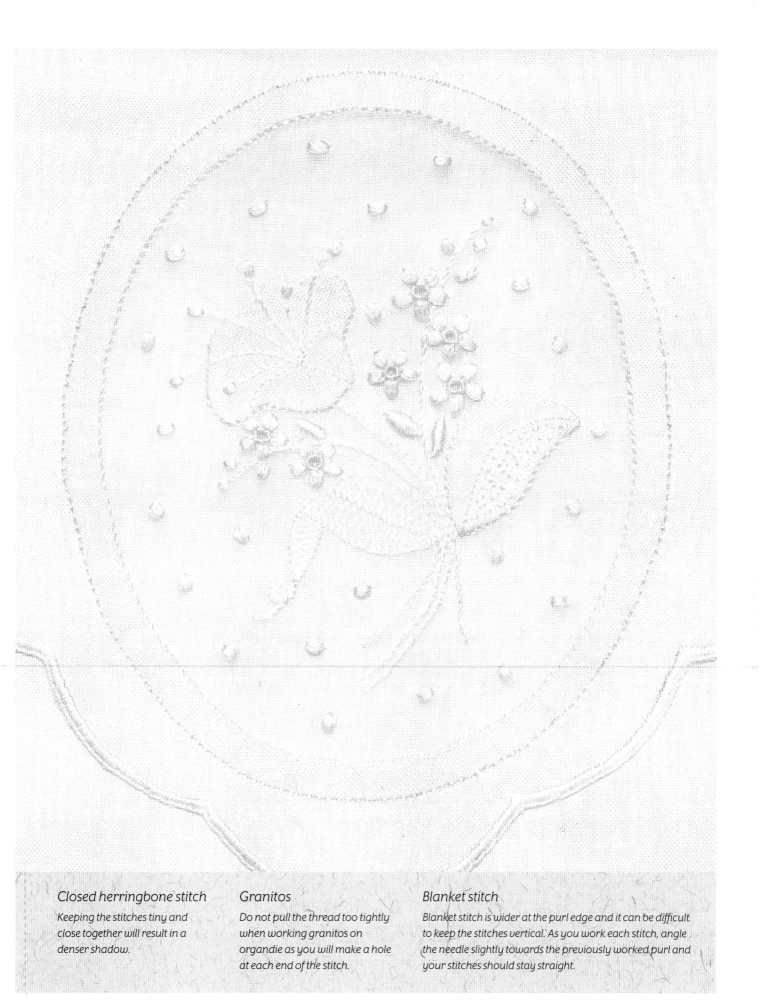

Closed herringbone stitch

Keeping the stitches tiny and close together will result in a denser shadow.

Granitos

Do not pull the thread too tightly when working granitos on organdie as you will make a hole at each end of the stitch.

Blanket stitch

Blanket stitch is wider at the purl edge and it can be difficult to keep the stitches vertical. As you work each stitch, angle the needle slightly towards the previously worked purl and your stitches should stay straight.

The Madeira Tradition

The Madeira islands are part of Portugal and consist of four land masses that lie approximately 800km off the west coast of Africa. Madeira is the largest of these islands.

The spectacular scenery and sunny climate are much loved by the many tourists who flock to the islands every year and Madeira is often referred to as the 'pearl of the Atlantic'.

Embroidery has always been part of the island's cultural history. Through the intervention of the English, Germans and Americans, Madeira work has become known around the world and prized for its fineness and the artistry of its designs.

During the 1850s, Elizabeth Phelps, noticed that the women of Madeira were very proficient with a needle and thread and she asked that they stitch some pieces that she sent home to England. She introduced the techniques of broderie anglais and from this, a cottage industry grew. German entrepreneurs saw the potential of high quality embroidered goods and broadened the industry to cater for a world market.

By 1900, the industry employed thousands of workers and continued until the outbreak of World War I. During the period 1916 to 1925, the industry suffered a serious decline.

IMPERIAL LINENS

In 1925, Charles Rolland and Leo Behrens formed Imperial Linens, choosing the golden crown as the symbol of their new company.

The embroidery designs and styles had not changed over the years, so Charles Rolland travelled to Europe to source new fabrics and techniques: appliqué and coloured threads from France, organdie from Switzerland, shadow work from Italy and cutwork from Spain.

The Imperial Linen Company adopted these techniques and developed them into the style that we now know as Madeira Embroidery.

Imperial used the best designs, finest materials and employed only the most skilled workers to complete each piece. Sadly, the Imperial Linen Company closed its doors for the last time in 2001.

THE HOUSE OF MARGHAB

The house of Marghab was established in 1933 by Emile Marghab and his wife Vera.

The embroiderers who worked for Marghab were registered and graded according to their competency. Without a registration card, they would not receive any work. They were paid by the stitch and the highest paid stitch was the scalloped buttonhole.

Marghab are considered to be the very finest of all Madeira linens and are sought-after collector's items. There are several pieces included in the permanent collection of the Metropolitan Museum of Art in New York City. The house of Marghab produced linens until the late 1970s.

THE EMBROIDERY

Embroidery in Madeira is still a cottage industry. Designs are applied to the fabric in the factory then collected by an agent, who distributes the work to the embroiderers. Women work at home on the pieces, then they are returned to the factory for finishing. Because the stitching is done in the home, the stitches and techniques are passed down through generations and a young child will learn to stitch from her mother or grandmother. When she becomes proficient, the young embroiderer will be registered and supplied with work.

In the early 1920s, the Embroidery Guild (Gremio) was founded to establish wages, benefits and set standards for the industry. Pieces to be sold have to pass inspection and are marked with a silver foil tag. This tag guarantees that the embroidery has met the most stringent quality standards.

MADEIRA PIN STITCH

As this stitch is worked, tiny holes are created when the vertical threads in the fabric are pulled together. It is important to maintain a firm, even tension on the thread throughout.

A finger shield is recommended for protecting the finger of your left hand as the needle passes through to the back of the fabric.

This step-by-step shows the authentic Madeira method for working pin stitch.

We used cream fabric instead of organdie and contrasting thread for photographic purposes.

1 Work a small backstitch on the back to secure the thread, ensuring it does not show on the front.

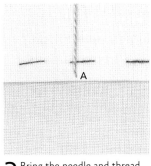

2 Bring the needle and thread to the front at A.

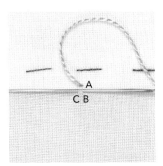

3 Take the needle from B to C on the cream fabric. B is directly below A.

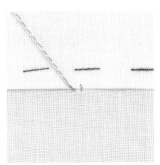

4 Pull the thread through.

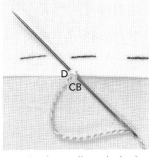

5 Take the needle to the back at B and across to D.

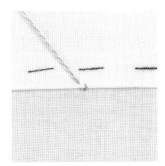

6 Pull the thread through firmly to open the holes. Completed first stitch.

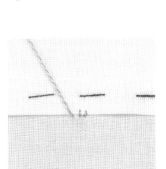

7 To begin the second stitch, take the needle to the back at C and re-emerge at E, a few fabric threads away from C.

8 Pull the thread through.

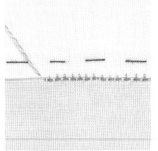

9 Repeat step 5. Pull the thread through firmly. Continue working stitches in this manner.

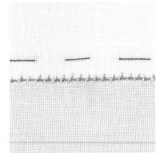

10 To end off, take the thread to the back and secure. Completed pin stitching.

GRANITOS

These tiny stitches are quick and easy to do. They can create different effects depending on the number of stitches worked and the thread used. Each granitos is worked with the fabric folded over the index finger of the other hand, using the same two holes in the fabric.

1 Bring the thread to the front and work a tiny backstitch.

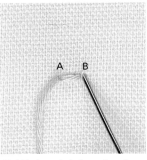

2 Work a stitch from A to B. Re-emerge at A and take the needle to the back at B through the same holes in the fabric.

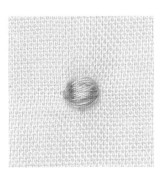

3 Work stitches into the same two holes until the desired size is achieved. Take to the back and secure.

Sweet Strawberry

DEBORAH LOVE

Traditional Mountmellick stitches and motifs have been used to create this captivating tablecloth.

Delightful strawberry plants, complete with flowers and fruit, intertwine around the inner border. Stitched onto white satin jean with matte white cotton threads, the rich texture of the embroidered surface contrasts beautifully with the smooth background. A decorative outer border and deep knitted fringe complete the cloth.

BEFORE YOU BEGIN

Read the complete instructions

See the pullout pattern for the embroidery design

All embroidery is worked with ONE strand of thread

THIS DESIGN USES

Bullion knot / Cable chain stitch / Chain stitch / Coral stitch / Cross stitch
Detached chain / Fishbone stitch / Fly stitch / French knot / Herringbone stitch
Knotted cable chain stitch / Lattice stitch / Long-armed feather stitch / Mountmellick stitch
Porcupine stitch / Satin stitch / Sawtooth blanket stitch / Stem stitch

The finished tablecloth measures 105 x 86cm wide (41³/₈ x 33¹/₈in) excluding the fringe

REQUIREMENTS

Fabric

1m x 137cm wide
(39½ x 54in) white cotton
satin jean

Supplies

50g ball 4-ply white knitting
cotton (3)

2mm (US no. 0 / UK no. 14)
metal knitting needles

20cm (8in) embroidery hoop,
inner ring bound

Tracing paper

Fine mechanical pencil

Fine black pen

Needles

No. 22 chenille

No. 24 chenille

No. 3 milliner's

Threads

No. 2 Mountmellick thread
A = white

No. 3 Mountmellick thread
B = white

PREPARATION FOR EMBROIDERY

Launder the fabric to remove any
sizing and to pre-shrink before
beginning the embroidery.

TRANSFERRING THE DESIGN

Join the required number of sheets of
tracing paper to create a 90 x 110cm
wide (35½ x 43in) piece. Using a
ruler and pencil, divide the piece into
quarters. Position the paper over the
embroidery design, aligning the ruled
lines with the placement marks and
tape in place. Trace the embroidery
design and border with the black
pen (diag 1).

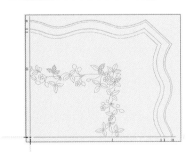

Repositioning the tracing paper for
each quarter, trace the embroidery
design and border onto the remaining
three quarters in the same manner.

Fold the fabric into quarters and
finger press the foldlines to mark the
centre. Centre the fabric over the
tracing, aligning the foldlines with
the placement marks.

Ensuring it is smooth, pin the fabric
securely in place along both sides of
the embroidery design and around the
border. Position one section at a time

over a lightbox or window
and lightly trace the embroidery
design and border with the fine
mechanical pencil.

EMBROIDERY

See pages 77–79 for the step-by-step instructions for working knotted cable chain stitch, Mountmellick stitch and porcupine stitch.

Use the no. 22 chenille needle when working with the no. 3 Mountmellick thread and the no. 24 chenille for the no. 2 Mountmellick thread. The milliner's needle is used for stitching the bullion knots.

All embroidery except the borders is worked in the hoop.

ORDER OF WORK

STEMS

Embroider the stems in coral stitch using **A**, working each section as the other elements progress.

STRAWBERRY FLOWER

The strawberry flowers are all embroidered in the same manner.

Working from the outer edge towards the centre, outline and fill each petal in chain stitch with **B**. Change to **A** and cover the petals with satin stitch, stitching from the outer edge towards the centre. For each petal, place the first stitch along the centre of the petal before filling one side at a time (diag 2).

Stitch a small detached chain sepal between each petal using the same thread. Fill the flower centre with five two-wrap French knots using **B**.

STRAWBERRY

Embroider all the strawberries in the same manner. Stitching from the base of the fruit to the top with **B**, work chain stitch along each side then along the centre of the berry (diag 3).

Fill the remainder of the shape with close rows of chain stitch in a similar manner. Change to **A** and scatter two-wrap French knots over the chain stitch for the seeds. Embroider the sepals at the top of the berry in detached chain with the same thread.

LEAVES

The leaves are embroidered in different stitch combinations, each repeated several times as indicated on the embroidery design.

Leaf A

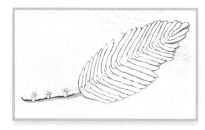

Starting at the tip, fill the leaf with closely worked long-armed feather stitch using **A**.

Leaf B

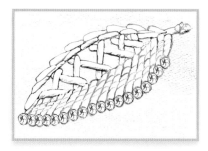

Working from the base to the tip, embroider the right-hand side of the leaf in porcupine stitch with **A**. Add a French knot at the end of each stitch along the outer edge. Embroider the left-hand edge in cable chain stitch and fill the remainder of the leaf with herringbone stitch.

Leaf C

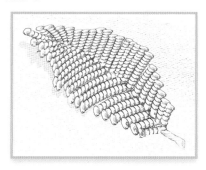

Using **A** and starting at the base, work bullion knots close together along one side, adjusting the lengths to cover the shape. Stitch the remaining side in the same manner, adding a knot at the point to form the tip.

Leaf D

Outline the leaf in stem stitch with **B**. Stitch evenly spaced French knots around the outer edge using the same thread. Change to **A** and work fly stitch along the vein.

Leaf E

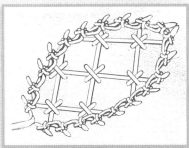

Outline the leaf in Mountmellick stitch with **B**, working each side from the base to the tip and ensuring the spokes of the stitches are facing outwards. Change to **A** and embroider the leaf filling in lattice stitch, couching the intersections with small cross stitches.

Leaf F

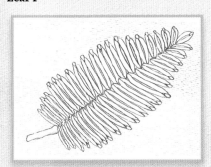

Using **B** and stitching from the base, fill each side with closely worked detached chains, bringing the needle to the front at the centre vein and taking it to the back on the outline. As you near the tip, gradually change the direction of the stitches to form the point.

Small leaves

Embroider the pairs of small leaves in fishbone stitch with **A**.

BORDER

The outermost border is embroidered in sawtooth blanket stitch with **B**, keeping the purl edge of the stitches along the outer edge. Work three long stitches to the second marked line followed by three half-length stitches, one long stitch and another three half-length. Repeat the sequence around the border. Stitch a French knot at the tip of each of the single long stitches and a detached chain above each group of three long stitches (diag 4).

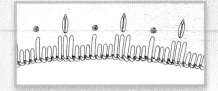

Using **A**, embroider five straight stitches to form a small star at each marked dot around the border. Keep each stitch approximately 4mm (³⁄₁₆in) long and take the needle to the back at the centre.

Embroider knotted cable chain stitch along each of the remaining two marked lines with **B**. Fill the space between these lines with herringbone stitch using the same thread.

FINISHING

Once the embroidery is completed, launder the cloth well to remove any pencil marks. Leave flat to dry. Steam press with the embroidered side facing down on a well-padded surface. Carefully trim the excess fabric as close as possible to the sawtooth blanket stitches on the outer border.

KNITTED FRINGE

Using all three balls of knitting cotton together, cast on 9 stitches.

Row 1. Pass the yarn around the needle to create a yarn over (make 1), knit 2 together, knit 1, make 1, knit 2 together, knit 1, make 1, knit 2 together, knit 1.

Repeat this row until the strip is long enough to fit around the edge of the cloth. Cast off the first 5 stitches.

Unravel the remaining 4 stitches to create the fringe. Neatly handstitch the short ends of the knitted lace together, incorporating the tails of the knitting cotton into the lace section of the fringe.

Attaching the fringe

Beginning at the join, hand whip the non-fringed edge of the knitted lace to the sawtooth blanket stitch border, stitching into the purl edge of the blanket stitches.

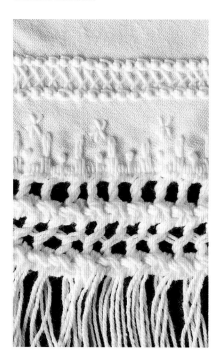

PORCUPINE STITCH

This stitch is formed by wrapping a straight stitch. For the Mountmellick tablecloth, it is worked in a row to create a textured filling for some of the leaves.

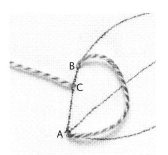

1 Bring the thread to the front at A. Take the needle to the back at B and emerge at C.

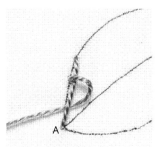

2 Pull the thread through. Wrap the long stitch by taking the thread over and under the stitch in a clockwise direction.

3 Pulling each wrap snugly, work a further 4–5 wraps. Take the needle to the back at A.

4 Repeat steps 1–3 to fill one half of the leaf, adjusting the spacing and direction of the stitches as required.

KNOTTED CABLE CHAIN STITCH

This stitch is a variation of cable chain stitch, with a coral knot added between each chain.

1 Emerge at A and hold the thread along the line.

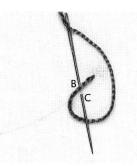

2 Take a small stitch under the line and the laid thread from B to C. The loop is under the needle tip.

3 Pull through, forming a coral knot. Slide the needle upwards under the first stitch.

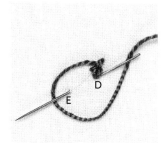

4 Loop the thread to the right. Take a stitch from D to E, emerging inside the thread loop.

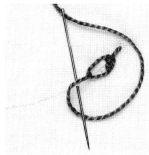

5 Pull through, forming a chain. Work a coral knot following step 2.

6 Pull through. Slide the needle upwards under the stitch between the chain and the knot.

7 Pull through. Work a second chain repeating step 4.

8 Repeat steps 5–7 to the end of the row, finishing with a coral knot. Take the needle to the back between the last chain and coral knot.

MOUNTMELLICK STITCH

The appearance of this traditional stitch is easily altered by spacing the stitches further apart and extending the stitch to the side.

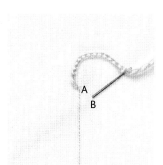

1 Emerge at A. Take the needle to the back at B, below and to the right of A.

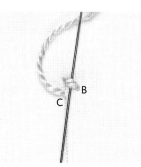

2 Emerge at C, to the left of B. Slide the needle downwards under the first stitch.

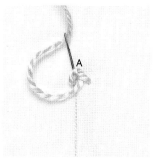

3 Pull the thread through. Loop the thread to the left and take the needle to the back at A.

4 Pull through, leaving a loop. Re-emerge at C, inside the thread loop.

5 Pull the thread through until the loop lies snugly against the emerging thread.

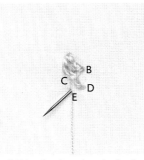

6 Take the thread to the back at D, below B, and emerge at E, below C.

7 Loop the thread to the left and slide the needle downwards under the second stitch.

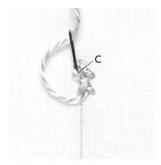

8 Pull through and loop the thread to the left. Take the needle to the back at C, inside the previous stitch.

9 Pull through, leaving a loop. Re-emerge at E, inside the loop.

10 Pull the thread through until the loop lies snugly against the emerging thread.

11 Repeat steps 6–10 to the end of the row. Take the needle to the back just over the last loop.

Sense of Place

LUZINE HAPPEL

Traditional folk motifs, tulips, hearts and
sunflowers are stitched with symmetrical
precision around the centre of this beautiful
cloth. Employing surface and drawn thread
work techniques, this superb example
of Schwalm embroidery has its origins
centuries ago in rural Germany. The elegant,
subtle colour scheme enhances the varied
texture of the stitches, creating a timeless
accessory for any dining occasion.

History of Schwalm

Schwalm whitework is a distinctive and traditional style of embroidery originating about two hundred years ago from the Schwalm district of the Hesse region in Germany. Worked on high thread count, evenweave linen, the designs consist of large motifs of simple shapes such as tulips, hearts, circles and birds. The motifs are bordered by coral stitch, chain stitch and sometimes other ornamental stitches and filled with a wide variety of drawn thread stitches.

BEFORE YOU BEGIN

Read the complete instructions and pullout pattern

See the pullout pattern for the embroidery designs

All embroidery is worked with ONE strand of thread

THIS DESIGN USES

Blanket stitch / Blanket stitch pinwheel / Chain stitch / Coral stitch
Diagonal cross filling stitch / Double bar satin stitch blocks / Four-sided stitch
Greek cross filling stitch / Honeycomb filling stitch / Needleweaving - five staggered rhombus
Peahole corner / Peahole hem / Satin stitch / Satin stitch - diagonal step / Single faggot stitch
Square eyelets / Wave stitch

The finished cloth measures 85cm (33½in) square

The finished embroidered design measures 38cm (15in) square

REQUIREMENTS

Fabric
1m (40in) square of ivory
36-count evenweave linen

Supplies
12.5cm (5in) embroidery hoop
Tracing paper
Fine tip black felt pen
Fine tip water-soluble fabric
marker
Embroidery scissors

Needles
No. 24 chenille
No. 26 chenille
No. 26 tapestry

Threads
DMC Broder Spécial no. 16
A = ecru (2 skeins)
DMC Broder Spécial no. 20
B = ecru (4 skeins)
DMC Broder Spécial no. 25
C = ecru (3 skeins)
DMC Broder Spécial no. 30
D = ecru
DMC Cordonnet no. 40
E = ivory

PREPARATION FOR EMBROIDERY

PREPARING THE FABRICS

Cut the fabric 93cm (36⅜in) square, by removing a fabric thread in each direction and cutting precisely along the drawn thread lines. Neaten the edges with overcasting by hand using white machine sewing thread to prevent fraying.

The overcasting remains inside the folded hem when constructed.

Fold the fabric in half in each direction and lightly finger press the folds. Using a light-coloured machine sewing thread, tack along the foldlines, following a fabric thread. Measure 20cm (7⅞in) from the centre and tack a parallel line in each direction to create a 40cm (15¾in) square (diag 1).

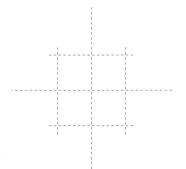

Using the water-soluble fabric marker, lightly rule a diagonal line from the

centre to each corner of the inner square and tack along these lines as before (diag 2).

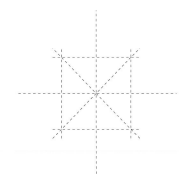

TRANSFERRING THE DESIGN

Using the black pen, trace the embroidery design and placement

marks for the side of the design onto tracing paper. Trace the corner motif and placement marks onto a separate piece in the same manner. Tape the side tracing to a flat surface and place the linen over the tracing. The tracing will show through the fabric. Aligning the placement marks with the centre and outer tacked lines of the square, pin the linen to the tracing to hold it accurately in place. Lightly trace the design using the fabric marker. Remove the pins, rotate the fabric and transfer the embroidery design to the remaining three sides of the square in the same manner. Transfer the corner motifs in a similar manner, using the diagonal tacked lines as a guide for placement. Remove all tacking threads.

> **NOTE**
>
> *It is important not to launder or soften the linen before stitching. Press the fabric with a hot dry iron only.*
>
> *Pay careful attention when positioning the linen over the tracing. The design must be aligned accurately with the fabric grain to ensure the drawn thread fillings will be straight.*

EMBROIDERY

See pages 88–97 for step-by-step instructions for working the drawn thread stitches.

Use the no. 24 chenille needle for working the coral stitch, blanket stitch and satin stitch. Use the no. 26 chenille needle when working the chain stitch outlines. Use the tapestry needle for all filling and drawn thread stitches.

The drawn thread embroidery is worked in the hoop unless otherwise specified.

ORDER OF WORK

SURFACE EMBROIDERY

Complete all outlines and surface embroidery first, as this helps to stabilize the fabric before cutting and withdrawing threads for the filling patterns. The motifs are embroidered in the same manner on each side of the design.

Motif outlines, stems and tendrils

Begin each thread by working a few running stitches towards the starting point (diag 3).

As you work the coral stitches back along the design line, the running stitches will be covered and the thread secured.

Embroider the large and small sunflowers, large and small tulip flowers, large leaf shapes, baskets, hearts, trefoil flowers, stems and tendrils with coral stitch using **A**. For the large tulip flowers, also outline each centre petal with coral stitch.

Large and small sunflowers

Using **B**, secure the thread and bring it to the front, close to the coral stitch outline. Work a blanket stitch scallop, using the same centre hole for each stitch, to fill the shape. Embroider the remaining petals in the same manner.

Stitch a blanket stitch pinwheel at the marked position above each large sunflower for the bud.

Tiny daisies

Work a blanket stitch scallop to fill each petal using **B**. Stitch a blanket stitch pinwheel at the centre of each daisy.

Small sunflower leaves

Using the same thread and beginning at the base of one leaf, bring the needle to the front at the centre line and work blanket stitches along the length of one side. Continue around the leaf tip and down the remaining side. Stitch the leaves at the base of the remaining small sunflowers in the same manner.

Small leaves

These leaves are found on the small tulips, large sunflowers, along the inner edge of the large tulip leaves and on the trefoil flowers.

Fill the leaves with closely worked satin stitches using **B**. For leaves lying to the right of a stem, begin stitching the lower half of the leaf at the base from the outline towards the leaf centre. Work a longer stitch at the leaf tip, and then stitch the remaining half from the tip towards the base. For leaves lying to the left of a stem, begin stitching at the base from the centre towards the leaf outline. Work the upper half first before completing the lower half.

Chain stitch reinforcing

Using **C**, work small chain stitches over three fabric threads each, just inside the coral stitch outlines of the motifs excluding the tiny daisies. Start and finish each row at the corner points for all motifs.

DRAWN THREAD FILLINGS

The filling stitches are worked over a grid prepared by carefully cutting and withdrawing threads. The work is then mounted, right side facing up, in the hoop. Take care not to distort the grain of the fabric when placing the fabric in the hoop. Remove the work from the hoop after completing the filling stitches in one area, before preparing the next grid of cut and drawn threads.

Large tulips–centre petal

Working from the back of the fabric at the widest point of the centre petal, lift a horizontal thread with a needle and carefully cut it (fig 1).

wrong side

Withdraw the thread to the left and right until you reach the chain stitch border (fig 2).

wrong side

Holding the withdrawn ends perpendicular to the fabric, carefully cut each thread close to the linen with embroidery scissors. Count three horizontal fabric threads above this first cut thread and cut and withdraw the fourth thread in the same manner as before. Repeat this process above and below the previous withdrawn threads, leaving a small area of intact fabric at the upper and lower sections of the shape (fig 3).

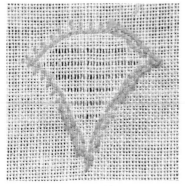

wrong side

Using **C** in the tapestry needle, and beginning on the right-hand side, fill the shape with wave stitch following the instructions on page 88. Pull the stitches snugly, but not tightly, so that tiny holes are created.

Small tulips

Beginning at the lower edge and working from the wrong side, cut and withdraw every fourth thread in the same manner as before, including the pointed upper petals (fig 4).

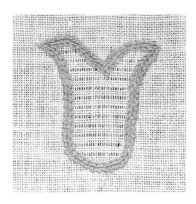

Using **C**, work honeycomb filling stitch to fill in the shape following the instructions on page 89.

Small sunflowers

Working from the wrong side of the fabric, cut and withdraw the tallest vertical thread within a small sunflower centre. Cut and withdraw a thread at the widest horizontal point as before. Cut and withdraw every fourth fabric thread in each direction over the entire centre, avoiding threads adjacent to the chain stitch border (fig 5).

Using **C**, work diagonal cross filling stitch to fill the shape following the instructions on pages 89 and 90.

Basket

Working upwards from the lower edge of the basket on the wrong side, cut and withdraw the fourth horizontal thread. Cut and withdraw the centre vertical thread. Create a grid in the same manner as for the small sunflower centres.

Embroider four-sided stitch across the basket using **C** following the instructions on pages 90 and 91.

Large leaves

Right-hand leaf

Working from the wrong side, cut and withdraw a vertical thread from the centre of the leaf shape, and the fourth horizontal thread from the top. Create a grid in the same manner as the basket. Using **B**, embroider satin stitch bars over the grid with a diagonal step following the instructions on page 91.

Left-hand leaf

Prepare the withdrawn thread grid for the leaf in the same manner as the right-hand leaf. Fill the leaf with rows of diagonally stepped satin stitches using the same thread, ensuring they are a mirror image of the right leaf.

Large tulips–outer petals

Working from the wrong side, cut and withdraw the centre vertical thread and the fourth horizontal thread from the base of a tulip. Create a grid in the same manner as the large leaves. The petals will be filled with a combination of two filling stitches.

Using **C**, bring the needle to the front through the centre hole at the base of the shape. Work rows of square eyelets forming a chequerboard pattern following the instructions on page 92.

The open thread framework created when drawing out threads in both directions, such as the small sunflowers, is known as a Limet. The name comes from the Latin words limes and limitis, relating to boundaries, surveying and division of plots.

Stitch partial eyelets at the edges of the shape where required.

Changing to **B**, bring the needle to the front at the base, two spaces to the right of the centre eyelet. Work double bar satin stitch blocks through the remaining unfilled areas of the petals, following the instructions on page 92.

Trefoil flower

Cut and withdraw two fabric threads that cross at the central axis of a trefoil flower. Create a grid in the same manner as for the tulip petals.

Using **C**, bring the needle to the front in the hole at the centre top of the flower. Work rows of Greek cross filling stitch to fill the shape following the instructions on page 93.

Large sunflowers

These flowers are filled with open-work patterns, so named because half of the fabric threads are first removed, making the fabric light and airy.

Cut and withdraw the centre horizontal thread at the back of one large sunflower centre. Cut and withdraw a second horizontal thread adjacent to the first. Remove the two vertical centre threads. Mount the work in the hoop, wrong side facing up, before withdrawing any further threads, as the fabric's stability will

be compromised. Working outwards from the centre, continue cutting and withdrawing pairs of threads in each direction, leaving two threads uncut between the withdrawn pairs.

Using **D** and working from right to left, embroider single faggot stitch along diagonal rows of the grid, following the instructions on page 94. Your thread length should be double the required stitching distance, as threads can only be secured at the edge of the shape and not ended in the grid itself.

Count the squares formed by the grid to determine the centre. Begin needleweaving the five-staggered rhombus shape at the marked position using **B**. Leave the end of the thread at the front of the work and embroider the needleweaving following the instructions on pages 94 and 95. Referring to the stitch chart, fill one half of the circle at a time with needleweaving rhombus shapes, changing the direction of each. Secure the thread tails into the back of the weaving stitches.

Heart motif

Each heart is filled with an open work Greek cross filling stitch pattern.

Remove two pairs of threads that cross on the central axis just below the heart's centre point. Form a grid

by cutting and withdrawing pairs of threads outwards from the first threads in the same manner as for the large sunflower centres. Using **D**, stabilize the thread grid with single faggot stitch.

Each square block is made up of eight Greek cross filling stitches. Working from the right side of the fabric, stitch the first square of Greek cross filling stitch at the tip of the heart, referring to the instructions on page 93, and using **C**. Fill the heart with squares in the same manner referring to the close-up photograph for placement.

When your working thread becomes too short, wrap it around the grid threads to the edge of the shape. Secure and end off the thread through the border stitches. Begin the new thread in a similar way and work your way back to the previous stitching position by wrapping around thread bundles as before. This will ensure the Greek cross filling stitch squares remain clear and distinct patterns.

HEM

Preparation

Withdraw one fabric thread on all four sides 1cm (⅜in) from the outer edge.

Working from the wrong side, lift one thread 4cm (1⅝in) from the left-hand edge and mark with a pin 5.5cm (2³⁄₁₆in) up from the lower edge.

Cut the thread at the marked point (diag 4).

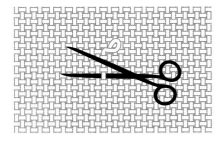

Withdraw the cut end towards the lower edge of the fabric leaving the tail 4cm (1⅝in) from the edge. Carefully withdraw the remaining cut end of the thread in the opposite direction, stopping 4cm (1⅝in) from the upper edge. Trim the thread, leaving a 1.5cm (⅝in) tail. Leave the thread tails on the wrong side of the fabric as they will be incorporated into the hem later.

Withdraw threads 4cm (1⅝in) from the fabric edge on the three remaining sides in the same manner.

Using **E** and the tapestry needle, embroider backstitch over four fabric threads along each of the inner withdrawn thread lines, working from the right side of the fabric. Pull the thread snugly, but not so tightly as to distort the fabric. When approaching the corner, slightly adjust the number

of threads in each bundle, finishing the last stitch exactly at the corner point. Continue working backstitches around the inner withdrawn thread lines in the same manner.

Working from the back of the fabric, withdraw a second line of fabric threads 7cm (2¾in) from the outer edge, in the same manner as before, leaving 1.5cm (⅝in) thread tails at each corner.

Count four fabric threads across, and cut the next thread 1.5cm (⅝in) from the adjacent drawn thread line. Withdraw the thread leaving the tail as before. Count across six fabric threads and cut and withdraw the seventh thread in the same manner. Count a further four fabric threads, cut and withdraw the fifth thread as before (diag 5).

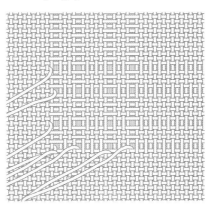

Withdraw the cut threads towards the opposite drawn thread line, leaving 1.5cm (⅝in) thread tails as before. Cut and withdraw threads along the remaining three sides in the same manner, leaving 1.5cm (⅝in) tails at the corners.

Peahole hem

When stitching the hem embroidery, hold the edge of the fabric in your hand and the bulk of the cloth away from you.

Working from the wrong side and using **E**, embroider four-sided hem stitch over four fabric threads between the two innermost withdrawn thread lines referring to the instructions on page 90. Stitch a second row of four-sided stitch over the next pair of withdrawn thread lines as before, taking care to work the stitches over the same vertical fabric threads as were used in the upper row.

Carefully cut and withdraw the six horizontal fabric threads between the two rows of four-sided stitch at each corner, following a straight line extension from the innermost withdrawn thread line in each direction (diag 6).

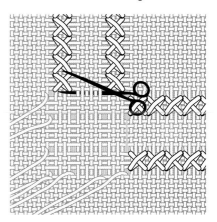

With the point of a needle, remove the short ends of the cut threads to the outer drawn thread line and lay them away from the open space created at the corner.

Carefully withdraw the six fabric threads between the two rows of four-sided stitches, one at a time.

Working from the wrong side, embroider the peahole hem between the rows of four-sided stitches with **E** following the instructions on page 96.

Peahole corners

Construct the hem and mitre the corners following the instructions in the pullout pattern before completing the peahole corners.

Mount the corner of the cloth in the hoop with the right side facing up to keep the corner fabric taut. Using **B** and the tapestry needle, work the peahole corner following the instructions on page 97.

CONSTRUCTION

See the pullout pattern.

WAVE STITCH

This stitch is used to fill the centre petal of the large tulip.
It creates a delicate lacy effect with zigzag stitches joining tiny regular holes in the fabric.
The stitches are worked from right to left as closely as possible to the border so that the chain stitches look as though they are lying on top of the filling pattern. To prepare the fabric withdraw every fourth horizontal thread (cut one, leave three) within the shape.

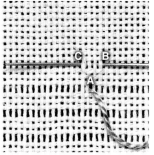

1 Row 1. Bring the thread to the front at A. Take the needle to back at B on the drawn line above and two threads to the right of A. Emerge at C four threads to the left.

2 Pull the thread taut. Take the needle back through A and pick up four threads to the left. Emerge at D.

3 Pull the thread taut. Take the needle from C to E, picking up four threads as before.

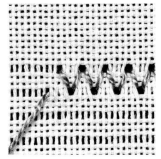

4 Pull the thread taut. Repeat steps 2 and 3 until reaching the left-hand side of the shape.

5 Row 2. Take the needle from F on the upper line to G on the drawn line below row 1.

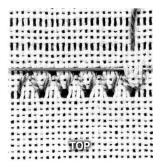

6 Turn the work upside down. Take the needle from right to left through the holes of the last wave stitch on row 1.

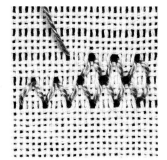

7 Continue working wave stitches across the row in the same manner as before.

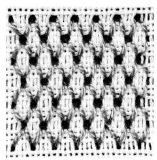

8 Work the third and following rows in the same manner to fill the shape.

HONEYCOMB FILLING STITCH

This dainty filling stitch decorates the small tulips. Beginning at the base, withdraw every fourth horizontal thread (cut one, leave three) across the tulip shape. We used contrasting threads for photographic purposes.

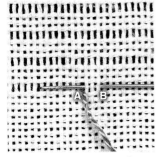

1 Bring the thread to the front at A. Take the needle to the back at B, three threads to the right. Re-emerge at A, wrapping the thread bundle.

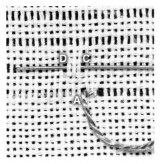

2 Pull the thread taut. Take the needle to the back at C on the drawn thread line, directly above A. Emerge at D, three threads to the left.

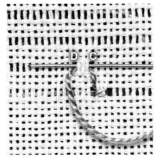

3 Pull the thread through. Take the needle from C to D again wrapping the thread bundle.

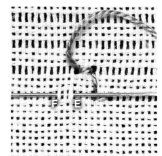

4 Pull the thread taut. Take the needle under three threads from E to F on the drawn line below.

5 Take the needle from E to F again to wrap the threads. Continue the stitch sequence in the same manner for the remainder of the row.

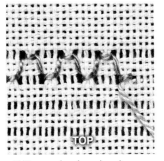

6 Secure the thread under a stitch on the wrong side. Turn the work upside down and re-emerge through the same hole.

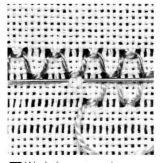

7 Work the next row in a similar manner, without wrapping the thread bundles that have already been wrapped.

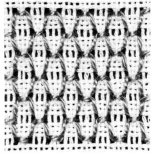

8 Work the third and subsequent rows in the same manner to fill the shape.

DIAGONAL CROSS FILLING STITCH

Diagonal cross filling stitch is worked quickly and is well suited for filling small motifs. This stitch is used to fill the centre of the small sunflowers. To prepare the fabric, withdraw every fourth thread (cut one, leave three) both vertically and horizontally within the shape to form a grid. We used contrasting thread for photographic purposes.

1 First row. Bring the thread to the front at A. Take the needle to the back at B and emerge at C, placing a vertical stitch over two thread groups.

2 Pull the thread taut. Take the needle to the back at D, two thread groups above C and emerge at E.

DIAGONAL CROSS FILLING STITCH

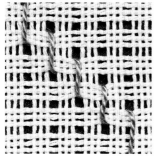

3 Continue working vertical stitches along the diagonal in the same manner.

4 Bring the thread to the front at F. Take the needle from G to H, placing a horizontal stitch over two thread groups.

5 Pull the thread taut. Take the needle from I to J for the second horizontal stitch.

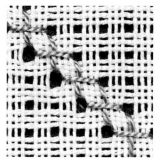

6 Continue working horizontal stitches along the diagonal in the same manner.

7 Second row. Bring the thread to the front at L, one thread group to the left of the first vertical stitch. Take the needle from C to K.

8 Complete the second row following steps 2–6, pulling the stitches taut to open out the holes in the fabric.

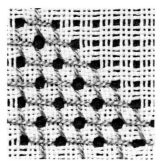

9 Continue in this manner to fill one half of the shape.

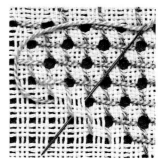

10 Turn the work upside down and stitch the remaining half from the centre in the same manner.

FOUR-SIDED STITCH

This stitch is also known as square open work stitch and four-sided open work stitch.
It is worked from right to left and used to fill the basket and along each side of the peahole hem.
To prepare the fabric for the basket withdraw every fourth thread (cut one, leave three) both
vertically and horizontally within the shape to form a grid.
We used contrasting threads for photographic purposes.

1 Bring the thread to the front at A. Take the needle from B to C.

2 Pull the thread taut around the thread group. Take the needle from A to D.

3 Pull the thread taut around the thread group. Take the needle from B to C.

4 Pull the thread taut. Take the needle from D to E.

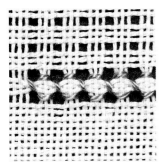

5 Pull the thread taut. Continue in this manner to the end of the row.

6 Turn the work upside down. Stitch the second row in the same manner, working a second stitch into the same holes as before.

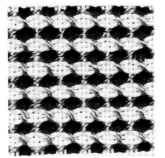

7 Continue in this manner to fill the shape.

SATIN STITCH BARS – DIAGONAL STEP

This stitch is used to fill the large leaves. To prepare the fabric, withdraw every fourth thread (cut one, leave three) both vertically and horizontally within the shape to form a grid.

1 **Right step.** Bring the thread to the front at the lower left of the shape (A). Take the needle to the back at B and emerge at C, one thread above A.

2 Repeat the previous step twice, moving up one thread each time and bringing the thread to the front at D after the last stitch.

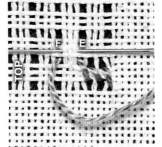

3 Pull the thread taut. Rotate the fabric 90 degrees to the left and take the needle from E to F.

4 Work two satin stitches parallel with the first stitch as before.

5 Rotate the fabric back and work three satin stitches over the next group of three fabric threads.

6 Continue in the same manner until the diagonal row is complete.

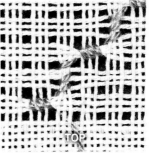

7 Turn the work upside down and bring the needle to the front one thread group below or to the right of the last block.

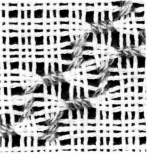

8 Work the next row in a similar manner to the first, alternating the vertical and horizontal bars.

SQUARE EYELETS

This stitch is combined with double bar satin stitch blocks to fill the large outer petals of the tulip. To prepare the fabric, withdraw every fourth thread (cut one, leave three) both vertically and horizontally within the shape to form a grid.

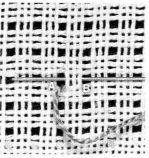

1 Bring the thread to the front at A. Take the needle from B to A.

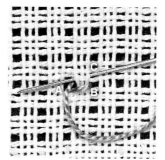

2 Pull the thread taut. Take the needle from C, one fabric thread above B, to A.

3 Pull the thread taut. Take the needle from D, one fabric thread above C, to A.

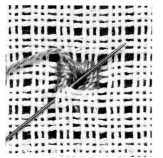

4 Pull the thread taut. Work further stitches one fabric thread apart, counter-clockwise, returning to the centre for each stitch.

5 Work the last stitch over the first stitch. Take the needle from B to E, three thread groups above.

6 Pull the thread through. Work a second square eyelet as before.

7 Stitch the following rows in a simlar manner to form a chequered pattern.

DOUBLE BAR SATIN STITCH BLOCKS

These are worked to fill in the remaining spaces in the fabric grid after the square eyelets have been worked.

1 Bring the thread to the front at A. Work a satin stitch over the thread group to the right.

2 Work a further five satin stitches above the first, each one thread apart. Take the needle from B to C.

3 Pull the thread through. Work another bar of six satin stitches over the thread group, to complete the first block.

4 Take the needle to the back between the two bars and emerge at D.

5 Continue in this manner, working pairs of satin stitch bars from the lower right to the upper left.

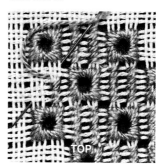

6 Turn the work upside down and work satin stitch bars in the same manner as before to fill the shape.

GREEK CROSS FILLING STITCH

Also known as rose stitch, this filling is used in the trefoil flower and the heart. The shape is filled by working rows of stitches diagonally. Withdraw every fourth thread (cut one, leave three) both vertically and horizontally within the shape to form a grid. In the heart, the filling stitch is worked over a base of single faggot stitch.

1 Bring the thread to the front at A. Loop the thread above and take the needle from B to A, keeping the thread under the tip of the needle.

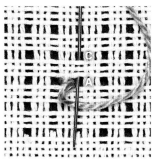

2 Pull the thread taut. Loop the thread to the right and take the needle from C to A, ensuring the thread is under the tip of the needle.

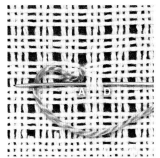

3 Pull the thread taut. Looping the thread below. Take the needle from D to A with the thread under the tip of the needle.

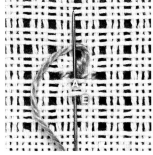

4 Pull the thread taut. Loop the thread to the left and take the needle from E to A, keeping the thread under the tip of the needle.

5 Pull the thread taut. Take the needle to the back at A, crossing over the fourth stitch.

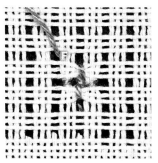

6 Bring the thread to the front through F, the hole diagonally to the left and above the first stitch.

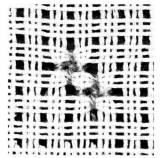

7 Work a second Greek cross filling stitch following steps 1–5.

8 Continue working Greek cross filling stitches to the end of the diagonal row.

9 Turn the work upside down. Stitch the next row in the same manner, pulling the stitches taut to create holes in the fabric.

SINGLE FAGGOT STITCH

This stitch is used to reinforce the fabric grid before working any further decorative stitches on large shapes, or as a decorative stitch on its own for smaller shapes.

Prepare the grid by withdrawing pairs of vertical and horizontal fabric threads (cut two, leave two). Rotate the fabric so the thread grid is on the diagonal and work the stitch across the grid from right to left on the wrong side.

1 Take the needle through the first hole near the right-hand edge at the widest section of the shape (A) and emerge at the next hole to the left (B).

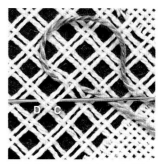

2 Pull the thread through. Take the needle from C to D on the diagonal line below.

3 Pull the thread through. Take the needle from B to E on the first diagonal line.

4 Pull the thread through. Continue this sequence to the opposite side of the shape and secure thread on outer edge.

5 Turn the work upside down. Beginning on the first completed row, work a second row in the same manner as the first.

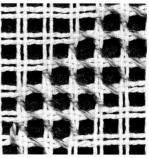

6 Continue working rows in the same manner across the shape, one half at a time, turning the fabric as required.

NEEDLEWEAVING – FIVE STAGGERED RHOMBUS

Needleweaving is worked from the right side of the fabric. Each square on the stitch chart represents a drawn thread square on the shape. In the centre of the sunflower, the needleweaving is worked over a base of single faggot stitch. Find the centre of the shape by counting the squares. The thread tail is left hanging at the front and will be secured later.

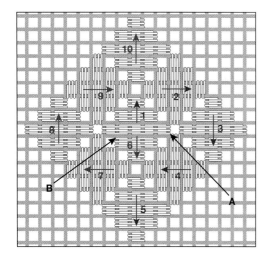

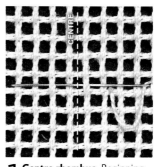

1 **Centre rhombus.** Beginning at the third square to the right of the centre, weave through the thread bundles from right to left under, over, three times.

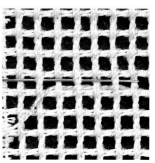

2 Pull the thread through. Weave from left to right through the previous squares in the opposite order.

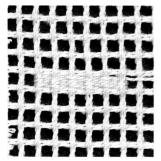

3 Continue weaving back and forth until you have woven three rows in each direction and the row of five squares is filled.

4 Take the needle to the back over the first thread bundle and emerge in the row above, one square closer to the centre.

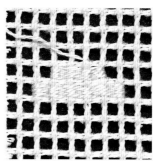

5 Weave as before, filling only three squares instead of five. Take the needle to the back and emerge at the centre square.

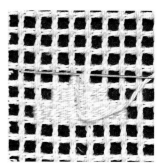

6 Weave back and forth over the two thread bundles to fill the centre square and complete the upper half of the centre rhombus.

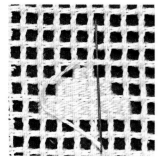

7 **Second rhombus.** Take the needle under the horizontal thread bundle on the right and emerge in next square above.

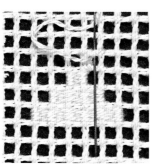

8 Working in a perpendicular direction to the previous stitching, weave to fill one square in the same manner as step 6.

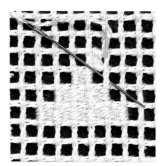

9 Take the needle from left to right under the vertical thread bundle below.

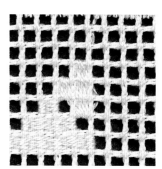

10 With the needle tip pointing away from you, take the needle under the next horizontal thread bundle to the right. Continue weaving, filling three squares.

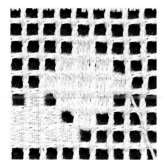

11 Continue weaving the rhombus shape over five, three and one square.

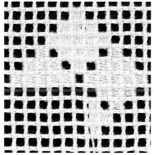

12 Continue working rhombus shapes alternating the weaving direction for each one.

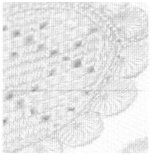

13 When filling the circular shape, weave the outer edges of the rhombus into the back of the chain stitch.

PEAHOLE HEM STITCH

This traditional Schwalm hem embroidery is worked between two rows of four-sided stitch on the outer edge of the cloth. The stitch is worked from corner to corner on the wrong side of the fabric.

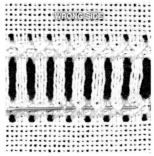

1 Secure the thread, sliding through the back of several four-sided stitches on the lower row.

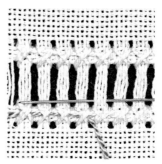

2 Take the needle from right to left under the first bundle of threads to the left.

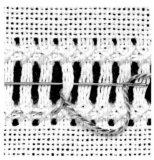

3 Pull the thread taut. Take the needle from right to left at the centre of the bundle.

4 Pull the thread taut. Take the needle from right to left through the back of the first two four-sided stitches above the bundle.

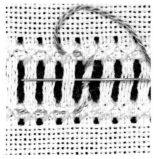

5 Pull the thread taut. Take the needle from right to left under the second thread bundle.

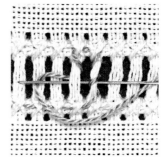

6 Take the needle from right to left under the first and second thread bundles keeping the thread under the tip of the needle.

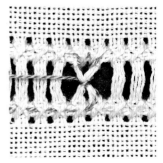

7 Pull the thread taut, pulling the thread bundles firmly together at the centre.

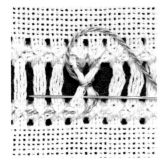

8 Take the needle from right to left under the lower half of the second thread bundle.

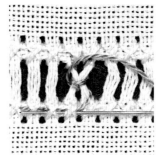

9 Take the needle from right to left through the back of the two, four-sided stitches below the second and third thread bundles.

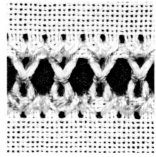

10 Continue steps 2–9 around the hem up to the next corner. Anchor the thread in the upper row of four-sided stitches to secure.

PEAHOLE CORNER

The peahole hem corners are worked after mitreing the cloth corners and securing the hem following the instructions in the pullout pattern. Carefully mount each corner of the cloth in the hoop before working the embroidery.

1 Secure the thread at the back of several four-sided stitches close to the corner and emerge just above the last four-sided stitch.

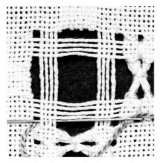

2 Take the needle from right to left under the thread bundle closest to the corner.

3 Pull the thread taut. Take the needle from right to left diagonally under the intersecting thread bundles.

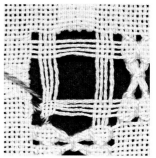

4 Pull the thread taut. Wrap the corner bundles twice more.

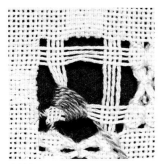

5 Keeping even tension, weave under and over the corner thread bundles for nine rows. Do not pull too tightly.

6 Wrap around the lower thread bundle twice more towards the inside corner.

7 Weave around the thread bundles at the new corner in the same manner as before.

8 Repeat steps 2–7 at each remaining corner. Secure the thread through the back of the weaving stitches and the four-sided stitches.

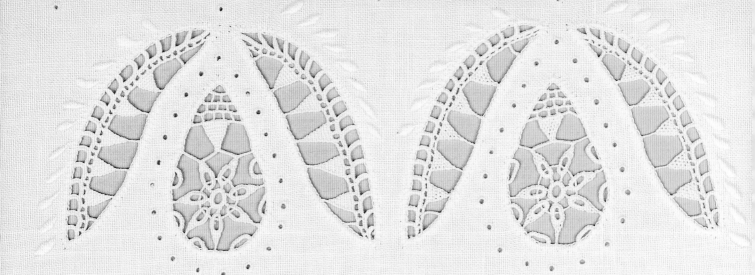

Stitch
Guide

STITCH GUIDE INDEX

BACKSTITCH

Work from right to left, keeping the stitches small and even in length. Take care to work through exactly the same hole at the end of a stitch as for the beginning of the previous stitch. Well-formed backstitches will look very similar to machine straight stitching.

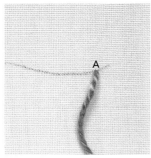

1 Mark a line on the fabric. Bring the thread to the front at A, approx 1.5mm (¹⁄₁₆in) from the right-hand end of the marked line.

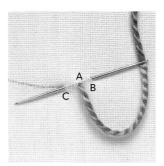

2 Take the needle into the fabric at the end of the line (B). Emerge at C, approx 1.5mm (¹⁄₁₆in) beyond A.

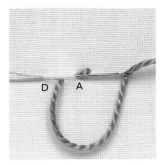

3 Pull the thread through. Take the needle to the back at A through the same hole in the fabric. Emerge at D, approx 3mm (¹⁄₈in) away.

4 Pull the thread through.

5 Continue working stitches across the line in the same manner, keeping them even in length.

6 To end off, take the thread through the hole at the beginning of the previous stitch. Secure on the back of the fabric.

BLANKET STITCH

Traditionally used to edge blankets, the basic stitch can be worked with many applications. Varying the spacing between the stitches creates different effects.

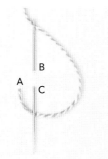

1 Bring the thread to the front at A. Take the needle from B to C. Ensure the thread lies under the tip of the needle.

2 Pull the thread through towards you until the stitch rests gently on the fabric.

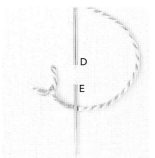

3 Take the needle from D to E at the same height as the previous stitch and parallel to it. Ensure that the thread is under tip of the needle.

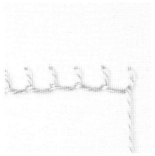

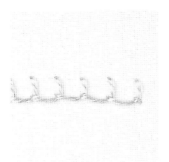

4 Pull the thread through. Continue to the end of the row in the same manner.

5 To end off, take the thread to the back just to the right of the last stitch. Completed blanket stitch.

BLANKET STITCH PINWHEEL

Often called blanket pinwheels, these simple yet effective flowers are formed using closely worked blanket stitches.

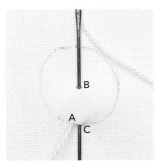

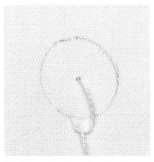

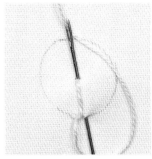

1 Draw a circle and mark the centre. Bring the thread to the front at A. Take the needle from B to C.

2 Place the thread under the needle tip. Begin to pull the thread through, pulling away from the circle.

3 Pull until the loop sits on the circle. Take the needle from the centre to the edge, again ensuring the thread is under the needle.

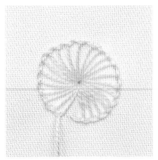

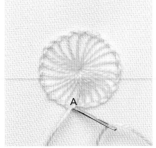

4 Continue working stitches around the circle, turning the fabric as you work.

5 Last stitch. Take the needle from B to A. With the thread under the needle, pull through. To anchor, take the needle to the back just over loop.

BULLION KNOT

To form a straight knot the number of wraps must cover the required distance plus an extra 1–2 wraps.

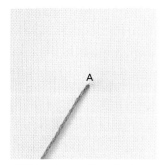

1 Bring the needle to the front at A. Pull the thread through.

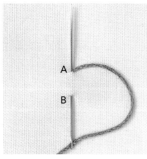

2 Take the needle to the back at B. Re-emerge at A, taking care not to split the thread. The thread is to the right of the needle.

3 Raise the point of the needle away from the fabric. Wrap the thread clockwise around the needle.

4 Keeping the point of the needle raised, pull the wrap firmly down onto the fabric.

5 Work the required number of wraps around the needle. Pack them down evenly as you wrap.

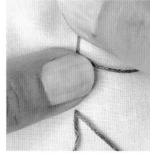

6 Keeping tension on the wraps with the left thumb, begin to ease the needle through the fabric and wraps.

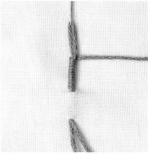

7 Continuing to keep tension on the wraps, pull the needle and thread through the wraps (thumb not shown).

8 Pull the thread all the way through, tugging it away from you until a small pleat forms in the fabric. This helps to ensure a tight even knot.

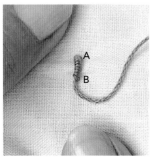

9 Release the thread. Smooth out the fabric and the knot will lie back towards B.

10 To ensure all the wraps are even, gently stroke and manipulate them with the needle while maintaining tension on the thread.

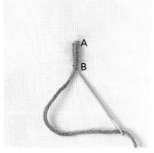

11 Take the needle to the back at B to anchor the knot.

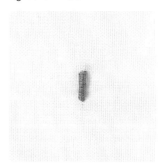

12 Pull the thread through and end off.

BUTTONHOLE STITCH

Also known as tailor's buttonhole stitch, true buttonhole stitch forms a row of firm twisted purls along the outer edge.

Rotate the work so that the outer edge is facing away from you and work stitches from left to right.

1 Bring the thread to the front a short distance from the edge.

2 Take the needle over the edge and emerge just next to the first stitch. Wrap the thread behind the eye then the tip of the needle.

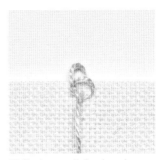

3 Begin to pull the thread through, pulling towards you.

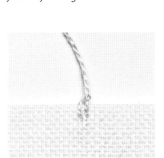

4 Pull the thread upwards so the loop slips along the stitch onto the edge.

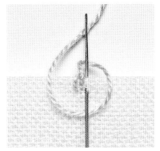

5 Take the needle over the edge and emerge next to the previous stitch. Wrap the thread as before.

6 Pull the thread towards you then upwards until the purl sits on the edge. Continue in this manner to the end of the row.

7 Detached buttonhole stitch. Work the stitches in the same manner over one or more straight foundation stitches.

CABLE CHAIN STITCH

A variation of chain, this stitch forms a row of chains linked with straight stitches. Make the chains slightly longer than the straight stitches.

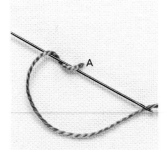

1 Bring the thread to the front at A and wrap around the needle as shown.

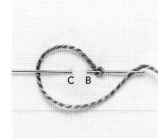

2 With the thread firmly around the needle, insert the needle at B and emerge at C. Keep the thread under the needle tip.

3 Pull the thread through to form the first stitch.

4 Continue working in this manner to the end of the row.

5 To end the row, anchor the last chain with a straight stitch and secure the thread at the back of the work.

CHAIN STITCH

This very versatile stitch can be used as an outline or in close rows as a filling stitch. Take care not to pull the loops too tight as they will lose their rounded shape.

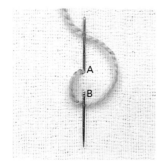

1 Bring the thread to the front at A. Take the needle from A to B, using the same hole in the fabric at A. Loop the thread under tip of the needle.

2 Pull the thread through until the loop lies snugly around the emerging thread.

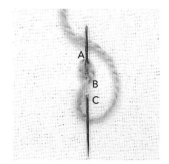

3 Take the needle through the same hole in the fabric at B and emerge at C. Ensure the thread is under the tip of the needle.

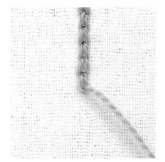

4 Pull the thread through as before. Continue working stitches in the same manner for the required distance.

5 To finish, work the last stitch and take the needle to the back of the fabric just over the loop.

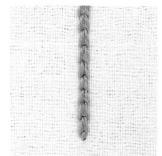

6 Pull the thread through to form a short straight stitch. End off the thread on the back of the fabric.

CLOSED HERRINGBONE STITCH

This stitch is also known as shadow work and is worked on the wrong side of the fabric.

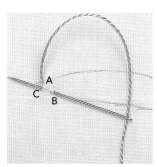

1 Bring the thread to the front at A. Take to back at B and emerge at C.

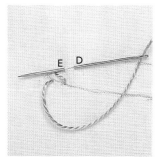

2 Pull the thread through. Take the needle to the back at D and emerge at E.

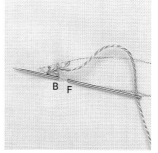

3 Take the needle to the back at F and emerge at B, through the same hole.

4 Continue filling the shape in the same manner.

CORAL STITCH

This knotted, linear stitch is excellent for joining seams. Similar in appearance to Palestrina stitch, it is less complex and easier to work.

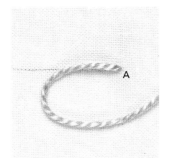

1 Emerge at A. Hold the thread along the line and loop it to the right.

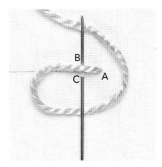

2 Take the needle to the back at B, just above the thread. Emerge at C, just below the thread.

3 Begin to pull the thread through.

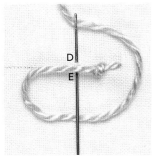

4 Pull until a knot forms. Repeat steps 1 and 2.

5 Pull the thread through as before to form a second knot.

6 Continue in this manner to the end of the row. To finish, take the needle to the back just after the last stitch.

COUCHING

Couching is used to secure a thread or stitch into a desired shape or outline. A thread or group of threads is secured to the fabric with tiny stitches, worked with a second thread.

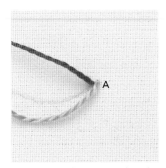

1 Bring the foundation thread to the front at A. Lay it along the design line. Bring a second thread to front just above the laid thread.

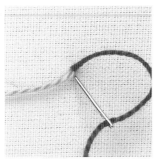

2 Take the second thread to the back over the laid thread. The stitch should hold the laid thread snugly but not squeeze it.

3 Pull the thread through forming a very short straight stitch. Emerge a short distance along the laid thread.

4 Continue couching the laid thread. At the end take it to the back. Finish couching and end off on the back.

CUT EYELET

These eyelets are stitched in a similar manner to pierced eyelets, however the fabric is cut rather than pierced.

1 Work a split stitch through the first stitch then bring the thread to the surface outside the outline.

2 Trim the tail close to the fabric. Using small sharp scissors, carefully cut the fabric into quarters at the centre of the shape.

3 Using the needle or the awl, fold each quarter of fabric under before beginning to overcast the section.

4 Complete the overcasting, trimming any excess fabric on the back. Secure the thread in the same manner as a pierced eyelet.

DETACHED BLANKET STITCH

This stitch creates a net over the fabric. To fill a shape, first work an outline of chain stitch or backstitch.

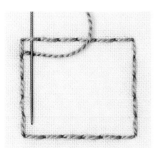  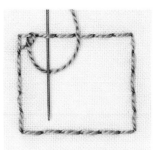 

1 Emerge at the left-hand side at the upper edge of the shape. Loop the thread to the right and slide the needle beneath the first outline stitch and over the loop. Do not pierce the fabric.

2 Pull the thread through to complete the stitch.

3 Work a second detached blanket stitch over the second outline stitch.

4 Continue across the row, working a detached blanket stitch into every outline stitch.

   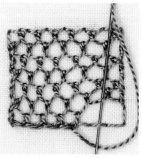

5 At the right-hand side, whip the outline twice, moving the thread to the position for the next row.

6 Work detached blanket stitch back across the shape, working each stitch into a loop from the previous row.

7 At the end of the row, whip the outline twice, moving the thread down for the next row.

8 Fill the shape with rows of detached blanket stitch, anchoring the thread around the outline at each side. Along the lower row, anchor each stitch under the outline.

DETACHED CHAIN

Also known as lazy daisy stitch. Detached chain stitch is a looped stitch, which can be worked alone or in groups.
It can also be used as a filling stitch with individual stitches placed at regular intervals over the space to be filled.

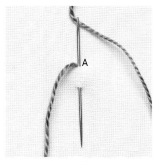

1 Bring the needle to the front at the base of the stitch (A). Take needle to the back as close as possible to A. Emerge at the tip of the stitch.

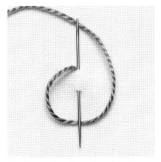

2 Loop the thread under the tip of the needle.

3 Keeping your left thumb over the loop, pull the thread through (thumb not shown). The tighter you pull, the thinner the stitch will become.

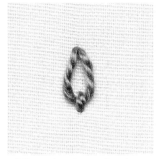

4 To anchor the stitch, take the thread to the back just over the loop. Completed detached chain.

DIAGONAL CABLE STITCH

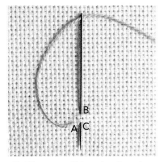

1 **First row.** Bring the thread to the front at A. Take the thread to the back at B and emerge at C.

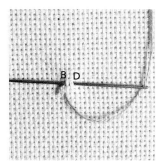

2 Take the thread to the back at D and re-emerge at B.

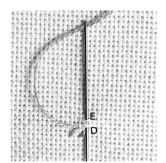

3 Take the thread to the back at E and re-emerge at D.

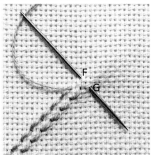

4 Continue working in this manner to the corner. Take the needle to the back at F and emerge at G.

5 Take the needle to the back at F again and emerge at H.

6 Take the needle to the back at I and re-emerge at G. Repeat steps 3–6.

7 **Second row.** Bring the thread to the front at J. Take it to the back at K and emerge at L.

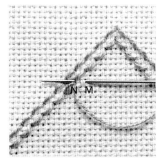

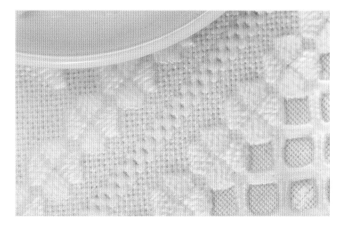

8 Take the needle to the back at M. Emerge at N. Work a second row of stitches inside the first.

9 Continue working the second row of cable stitch as before.

DIAGONAL CROSS FILLING STITCH

Diagonal cross filling stitch is worked quickly and is well suited for filling small motifs. To prepare the fabric, withdraw every fourth thread (cut one, leave three) both vertically and horizontally within the shape to form a grid.

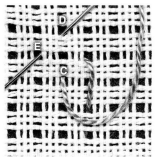

1 First row. Bring the thread to the front at A. Take the needle to the back at B and emerge at C, placing a vertical stitch over two thread groups.

2 Pull the thread taut. Take the needle to the back at D, two thread groups above C and emerge at E.

3 Continue working vertical stitches along the diagonal in the same manner.

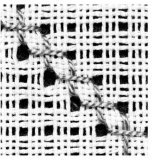

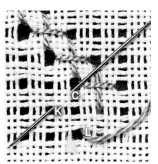

4 Bring the thread to the front at F. Take the needle from G to H, placing a horizontal stitch over two thread groups.

5 Pull the thread taut. Take the needle from I to J for the second horizontal stitch.

6 Continue working horizontal stitches along the diagonal in the same manner.

7 Second row. Bring the thread to the front at L, one thread group to the left of the first vertical stitch. Take the needle from C to K.

8 Complete the second row following steps 2–6, pulling the stitches taut to open out the holes in the fabric.

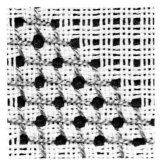

9 Continue in this manner to fill one half of the shape.

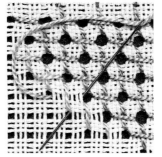

10 Turn the work upside down and stitch the remaining half from the centre in the same manner.

DIAGONAL DRAWN FILLING

This filling is worked in a similar manner to single faggot filling, with one fabric thread left between diagonal rows of stitching rather than fabric holes being shared between rows. This leaves a delicate cross of fabric threads within the opened holes created by the pulled stitches. Each stitch is worked over four fabric threads.

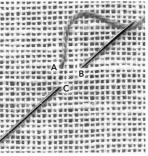

1 Row 1. Emerge at A. Take the needle from B to C.

2 Pull the thread taut. Take the needle from A to D.

3 Pull the thread taut. Take the needle from C to E.

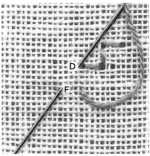

4 Pull the thread taut. Take the needle from D to F.

5 Pull the thread taut. Repeat the stitch sequence to the end of the row.

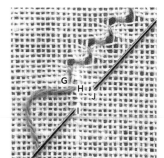

6 Row 2. Emerge at H, one thread across and down from G. Take the needle from I to J.

7 Pull the thread taut. Take the needle from H to L.

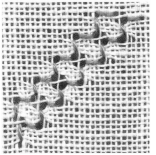

8 Pull the thread taut. Repeat the stitch sequence along the diagonal, in the opposite direction to row 1.

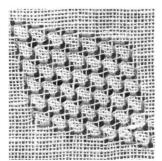

9 Continue working diagonal rows of diagonal drawn filling until the shape is filled, working partial rows where needed.

DOUBLE BAR SATIN STITCH BLOCKS

These are worked to fill in the remaining spaces in the fabric grid after the square eyelets have been worked.

1 Bring the thread to the front at A. Work a satin stitch over the thread group to the right.

2 Work a further five satin stitches above the first, each one thread apart. Take the needle from B to C.

3 Pull the thread through. Work another bar of six satin stitches over the thread group, to complete the first block.

4 Take the needle to the back between the two bars and emerge at D.

5 Continue in this manner, working pairs of satin stitch bars from the lower right to the upper left.

6 Turn the work upside down and work satin stitch bars in the same manner as before to fill the shape.

EYELET

These embroidered eyelets are the basis of traditional white-on-white broderie anglaise or Swiss embroideries. They are also used in Madeira and Venetian embroidery. An eyelet is a pierced hole that is surrounded by running stitches, then covered by short, regular overcasting stitches. The beauty of this technique is in the regularity of the stitches.

1 Mark a tiny circle on the fabric. Leaving a short tail, work a row of running stitches around the circle, leaving tiny stitches at the back.

2 Work a split stitch through the first stitch in the circle, then bring the thread to the front just outside the outline at A.

3 Trim the tail close to the fabric. Using an awl, pierce the fabric and open up the eyelet.

4 Take the needle down through the hole and emerge on the outer edge. Pull the thread firmly.

5 Continue working overcast stitches until two stitches from completing the circle. Work the final two stitches leaving them loose.

6 Take the needle through the two stitches and pull firmly. Snip the thread close to the stitching.

7 Using the awl, re-pierce the eyelet from the front and back. This helps to settle the thread and fabric.

8 Finished eyelet.

FISHBONE STITCH

This is a versatile filling or line stitch and can be worked with the stitches close together or spaced apart. It is particularly useful for working leaves and feathers.

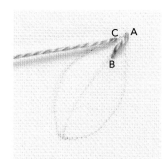

1 Bring the thread to the front at A. Take the needle to the back at B and emerge at C.

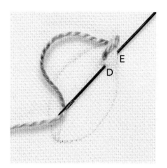

2 With the thread looped to the left, take the thread from D, just to the right of the centre line, to E.

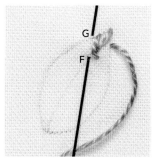

3 With the thread looped to the right take the needle from F, just to the left of the centre line, to G.

4 Continue working in this manner until the shape is filled.

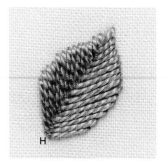

5 Take the thread to the back at H and secure.

FLY STITCH

Fly stitch is an open detached chain stitch with many possible variations.
It is worked in the shape of a 'V' or 'Y' depending on the length of the anchoring stitch.

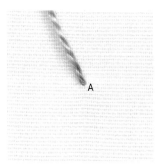 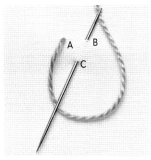 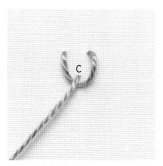 

1 Bring the thread to the front at A. This will be the left-hand side of the stitch.

2 Take the needle to the back at B and emerge at C. Loop the thread under the tip of the needle and to the right.

3 Hold the loop in place under the left thumb (thumb not shown). Pull the needle through until the looped thread lies snugly against C.

4 Take the thread to the back at the required distance below C to anchor the fly stitch. Completed fly stitch.

FOUR-SIDED STITCH

Four-sided stitch forms is an effective filling or linear stitch.

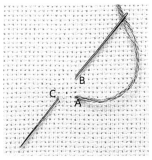 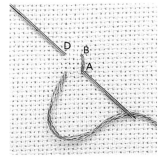 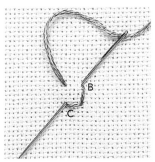

1 Bring the needle to the front at A. Take it to the back at B, four threads above A. Emerge at C, four threads below and four to the left.

2 Pull the needle through and insert at A. Bring to the front at D, four threads above and four to the left.

3 Insert the needle at B and re-emerge at C.

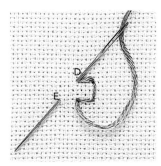 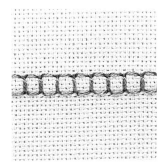 

4 Insert the needle at D and emerge at E, four threads below and four to the left.

5 Continue in this manner to the end of the row.

FOUR-SIDED STITCH
(Drawn thread)

This stitch is also known as square open work stitch and four-sided open work stitch. It is worked from right to left. To prepare the fabric withdraw every fourth thread (cut one, leave three) both vertically and horizontally within the shape to form a grid.

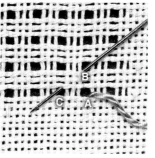

1 Bring the thread to the front at A. Take the needle from B to C.

2 Pull the thread taut around the thread group. Take the needle from A to D.

3 Pull the thread taut around the thread group. Take the needle from B to C.

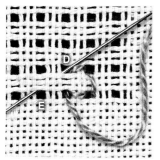

4 Pull the thread taut. Take the needle from D to E.

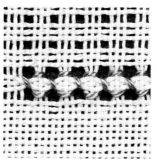

5 Pull the thread taut. Continue in this manner to the end of the row.

6 Turn the work upside down. Stitch the second row in the same manner, working a second stitch into the same holes as before.

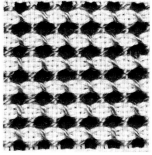

7 Continue in this manner to fill the shape.

FRAMED CROSS FILLING

Pairs of satin stitches worked in horizontal and vertical rows open out holes in the fabric with crosses formed from single fabric threads. Each stitch is worked over four fabric threads.

1 **Horizontal rows.** Work pairs of vertical satin stitches across the first row, leaving four fabric threads between each pair.

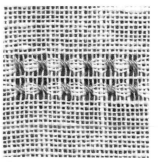

2 Leave one horizontal fabric thread. Work pairs of vertical satin stitches back across the row, aligning the stitches with the previous row.

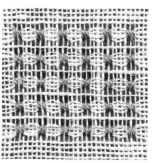

3 Work horizontal rows until the shape is full.

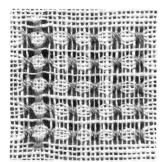

4 **Vertical rows.** Working from the upper to the lower edge, stitch pairs of horizontal satin stitches between the previous stitches.

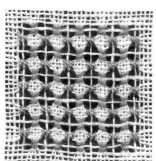

5 Continue working pairs of horizontal stitches down the remaining vertical rows to complete the filling.

FRENCH KNOT

A French knot is a raised stitch that can add wonderful textural qualities to your embroidery.
Traditionally, French knots were worked with only one wrap; however, today they are often worked with more than one wrap.
A large knot will look neater and be more secure if it is worked with more strands of thread rather than too many wraps.

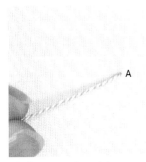

1 **One-wrap French knot.** Bring the thread to the front at A. Hold the thread firmly with your left thumb and index finger approximately 3cm (1¼in) away from the fabric.

2 Keeping the thread taut, take the needle behind the thread with your right hand and then the thread over needle with your left hand.

3 Still keeping the thread taut, twist the tip of the needle away from you and towards the fabric.

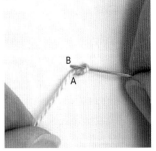

4 Take the tip of the needle to the back at B, approx 1–2 fabric threads away from A. Ensure it does not go through the fabric at A.

5 Pull the thread taut, sliding the knot down the needle and onto the fabric.

6 Push the needle through to the wrong side. As the eye passes through, place your left thumb over knot (thumb not shown).

7 Keeping your thumb on the knot, continue to pull the thread through until the loop disappears under your thumb.

8 Continue pulling until you feel the thread resisting. Move your thumb. Completed one wrap French knot.

9 **Two-wrap French knot.** Follow steps 1–3 above. Take the thread over the needle again slightly closer towards the tip than the first wrap.

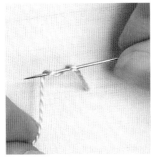

10 Keeping the thread taut, continue taking the thread around and under the needle until it is back on the side it started from.

11 Ensure the wraps lie close together by pulling on the thread.

12 Take the needle to the back and pull the thread through following steps 5–9 above. Completed two-wrap French knot.

GRANITOS

These tiny stitches are quick and easy to do. They can create different effects depending on the number of stitches worked and the thread used. Each granitos is worked with the fabric folded over the index finger of the other hand, using the same two holes in the fabric.

1 Bring the thread to the front and work a tiny backstitch.

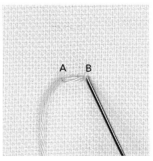

2 Work a stitch from A to B. Re-emerge at A and take the needle to the back at B through the same holes in the fabric.

3 Work stitches into the same two holes until the desired size is achieved. Take to the back and secure.

GRAPE

Each grape is worked with three strands of stranded cotton, each 1m (39in) in length. It is important to have enough thread to finish the grape without having to join it.

1 Wrap the threads twice around the skewer, leaving a 12cm (4¾in) tail.

2 Leaving the tail dangling, work detached blanket stitch over the threads to form a ring.

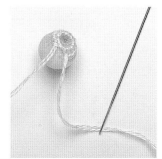

3 Put a small amount of glue on the top of a bead. Wait until it is tacky and place the ring over it.

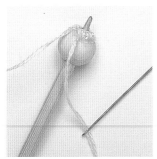

4 Insert the pointed end of the skewer into the hole at the base of the bead.

5 Begin working detached blanket stitch into the ring, covering the tail.

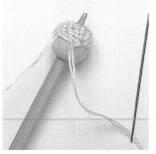

6 Increase the number of stitches at the widest part of the bead and decrease as you approach the base.

7 Remove the skewer to complete the stitching at the base.

8 Thread the tail and working thread into the needle and take through the hole in the base to the top, leaving at least 10cm (4in) of each thread.

9 **Attaching the grape.** Thread both tails into the needle and attach the grape securely at the marked position.

GREEK CROSS FILLING STITCH

Also known as rose stitch. This shape is filled by working rows of stitches diagonally. Withdraw every fourth thread (cut one, leave three) both vertically and horizontally within the shape to form a grid.

1 Bring the thread to the front at A. Loop the thread above and take the needle from B to A, keeping the thread under the tip of the needle.

2 Pull the thread taut. Loop the thread to the right and take the needle from C to A, ensuring the thread is under the tip of the needle.

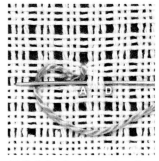

3 Pull the thread taut. Looping the thread below. Take the needle from D to A with the thread under the tip of the needle.

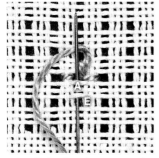

4 Pull the thread taut. Loop the thread to the left and take the needle from E to A, keeping the thread under the tip of the needle.

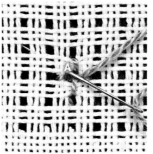

5 Pull the thread taut. Take the needle to the back at A, crossing over the fourth stitch.

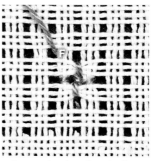

6 Bring the thread to the front through F, the hole diagonally to the left and above the first stitch.

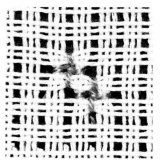

7 Work a second Greek cross filling stitch following steps 1–5.

8 Continue working Greek cross filling stitches to the end of the diagonal row.

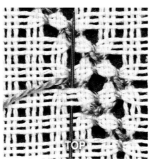

9 Turn the work upside down. Stitch the next row in the same manner, pulling the stitches taut to create holes in the fabric.

HEDEBO PICOT STITCH

Hedebo picots add a dainty finishing touch to the centre of needlelace arches formed from laid threads covered with Hedebo stitch.

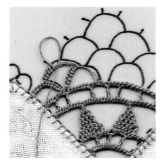

1 Begin to cover an arch of laid threads with Hedebo stitch. At the position for the picot, take the thread under the arch, leaving a loop.

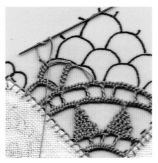

2 Place the needle through the loop and around the thread as shown, so that the thread is twisted twice around the needle.

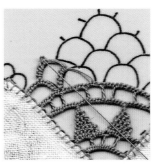

3 Pull the needle and thread through. Take the needle back through the base of the stitch to complete the picot and tighten the thread.

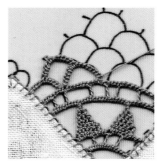

4 Complete the arch with Hedebo stitch and continue working as required.

HEDEBO STITCH

Also known as Hedebo buttonhole and Danish buttonhole, this knotted stitch is characteristic of Hedebo embroidery and is used to edge cut shapes.

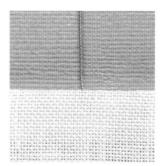

1 Secure the thread and bring it to the surface at the folded edge of the fabric.

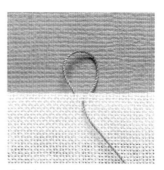

2 Take a stitch through the fabric and pull through leaving a small loop.

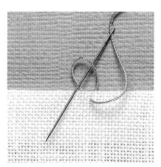

3 Take the needle through the loop, from back to front.

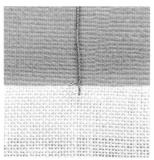

4 Pull the thread up until the knot tightens and the loop sits firmly.

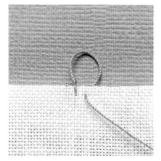

5 Make a second stitch and pull the thread through leaving a small loop.

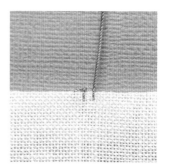

6 Take the needle through the loop, from back to front and pull the thread up as before.

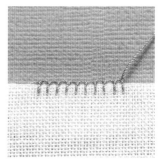

7 Continue working in this manner around the shape.

HERRINGBONE STITCH

This stitch is often used to work decorative borders and fillings. Space the stitches closer or wider apart according to the desired effect. Mark two lines to help keep your stitches even.

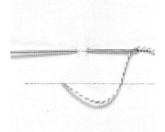

1 Emerge on the lower line. With the thread below, take the needle from right to left on the upper line.

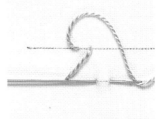

2 With the thread above, take the needle from right to left on the lower line. Keep the stitch length the same as the previous stitch.

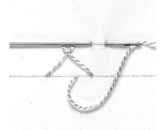

3 With the thread below, take the needle from right to left on the upper line.

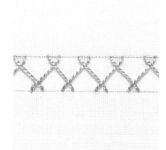

4 Continue working evenly spaced stitches, alternating between the lower and upper lines.

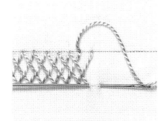

5 Closed herringbone stitch. Emerge in the same hole as the previous stitch.

HONEYCOMB FILLING STITCH

Beginning at the base, withdraw every fourth horizontal thread (cut one, leave three).

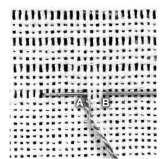

1 Bring the thread to the front at A. Take the needle to the back at B, three threads to the right. Re-emerge at A, wrapping the thread bundle.

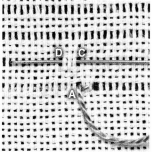

2 Pull the thread taut. Take the needle to the back at C on the drawn thread line, directly above A. Emerge at D, three threads to the left.

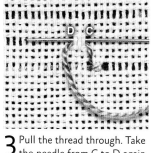

3 Pull the thread through. Take the needle from C to D again wrapping the thread bundle.

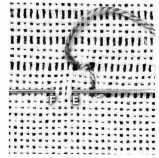

4 Pull the thread taut. Take the needle under three threads from E to F on the drawn line below.

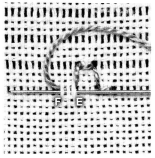

5 Take the needle from E to F again to wrap the threads. Continue the stitch sequence in the same manner for the remainder of the row.

6 Secure the thread under a stitch on the wrong side. Turn the work upside down and re-emerge through the same hole.

7 Work the next row in a similar manner, without wrapping the thread bundles that have already been wrapped.

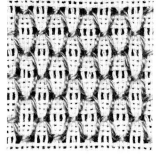

8 Work the third and subsequent rows in the same manner to fill the shape.

ITALIAN INSERTION STITCH

This decorative stitch is used to join seams.

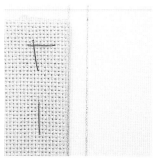

1 Place the side of the bag against one drawn line on the spacer so that the other drawn line is visible.

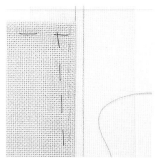

2 Tack firmly until reaching the tacking line representing the base.

3 Fold the fabric and spacer so that the top edges are even. Tack the remaining side to the second line on the spacer interfacing.

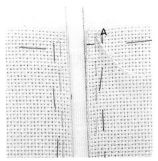

4 Italian insertion stitch. Bring the needle up at A, two threads in from the edge and two down from the top.

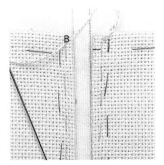

5 Take the needle from the back at B, two threads in from the edge and two down from the top.

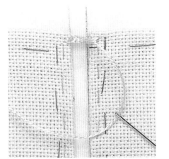

6 Repeat, working into the same holes. Work four detached blanket stitches from left to right across the loop.

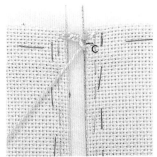

7 Work a blanket stitch on the right edge at C, two threads in from the edge and two threads down from the starting point.

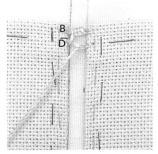

8 Work another blanket stitch on the left at D, four threads below B.

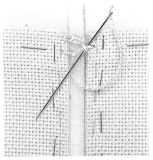

9 Work a detached blanket stitch around the centre of the blanket stitch on the right fabric edge.

10 Work three more stitches around the same stitch, working from left to right.

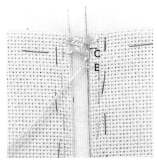

11 Work a blanket stitch on the right side at E, four threads below C.

12 Work a detached blanket stitch at the centre of the stitch on the left-hand side.

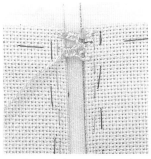

13 Work three more stitches around the same stitch, working from right to left.

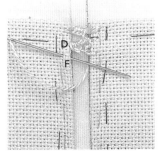

14 Work a blanket stitch on the left edge at F, four threads below D.

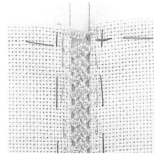

15 Continue in the same manner until reaching the base of the bag.

KLOSTER BLOCKS

Kloster blocks consist of five parallel stitches over a grid of four by four fabric threads. Each block is worked at a right-angle to the previous one.

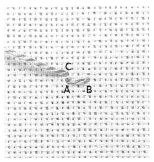

1 Bring the thread to the front at A. Take it to the back at B and bring it to the front at C.

2 Take the thread to the back at D and bring it to the front at E.

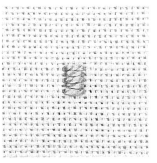

3 Continue until five stitches have been worked.

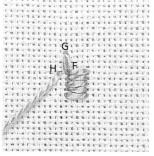

4 Bring the thread to the front at F and take it to the back at G. Emerge at H.

5 Continue until five stitches have been worked.

KNOTTED CABLE CHAIN STITCH

This stitch is a variation of cable chain stitch, with a coral knot added between each chain.

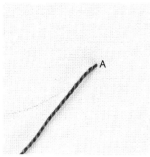

1 Emerge at A and hold the thread along the line.

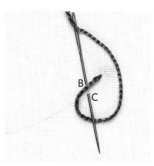

2 Take a small stitch under the line and the laid thread from B to C. The loop is under the needle tip.

3 Pull through, forming a coral knot. Slide the needle upwards under the first stitch.

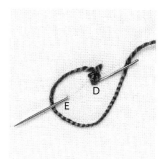

4 Loop the thread to the right. Take a stitch from D to E, emerging inside the thread loop.

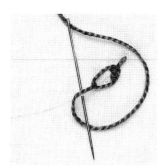

5 Pull through, forming a chain. Work a coral knot following step 2.

6 Pull through. Slide the needle upwards under the stitch between the chain and the knot.

7 Pull through. Work a second chain repeating step 4.

8 Repeat steps 5–7 to the end of the row, finishing with a coral knot. Take the needle to the back between the last chain and coral knot.

LEVIATHAN STITCH

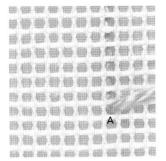

1 Secure the thread. Bring it to the front at A, on the upper left-hand side. This is the lower right-hand corner of the stitch.

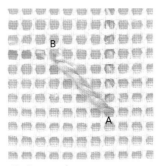

2 Crossing four intersections, take the needle to the back at B. This is the upper left-hand corner of the stitch. Pull the thread through.

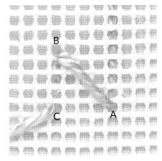

3 Emerge at C, four threads below B. Pull the thread through.

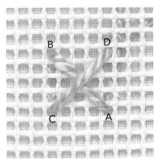

4 Crossing four intersections, take the needle to the back at D in the upper right-hand corner of the stitch. Pull the thread through.

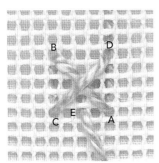

5 Emerge at E, halfway between A and C. Pull the thread through.

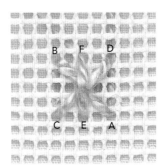

6 Crossing four threads, take the needle to the back at F, directly above. Pull the thread through.

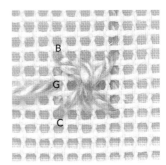

7 Emerge at G, halfway between B and C. Pull the thread through.

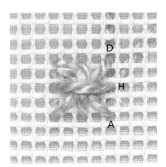

8 Crossing four threads to the right, take the needle to the back at H. Pull the thread through.

LINE OF PIERECED EYELETS

Use this method when you require a trail of eyelets. When working the first pass of overcasting stitches, skip across the point where the two circles touch. Stitch this when returning with the second pass of overcasting. This prevents having an unsightly lump of thread if this point is overcast twice.

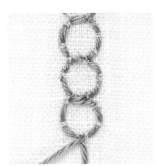

1 Work a line of running stitches around the outline in the shape of a figure eight.

2 Using the awl, pierce each eyelet before working the first edge.

3 Work the overcast stitches following the same path as the running stitches.

4 Complete the overcasting before securing the thread in the same manner as a pierced eyelet.

LONG-ARMED FEATHER STITCH

This variation of feather stitch can be used as an effective filling for leaf and petal shapes. Starting at the pointed end, work the first stitch with the tips together.

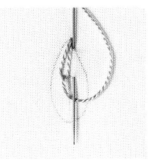

1 At the right-hand side take the needle to the back on the outline and emerge to the right of the centre line.

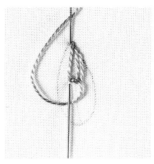

2 At the left-hand side take the needle to the back on the outline and emerge to the left of the centre line.

3 Continue working in this manner to fill the shape.

MADEIRA PIN STITCH

As this stitch is worked, tiny holes are created when the vertical threads in the fabric are pulled together. It is important to maintain a firm, even tension on the thread throughout.

A finger shield is recommended for protecting the finger of your left hand as the needle passes through to the back of the fabric.

This step-by-step shows the authentic Madeira method for working pin stitch.

We used cream fabric instead of organdie and contrasting thread for photographic purposes.

1 Work a small backstitch on the back to secure the thread, ensuring it does not show on the front.

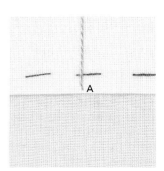

2 Bring the needle and thread to the front at A.

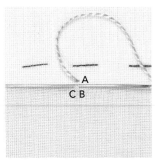

3 Take the needle from B to C on the cream fabric. B is directly below A.

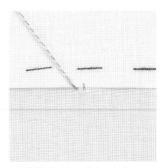

4 Pull the thread through.

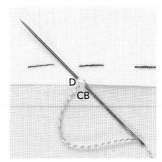

5 Take the needle to the back at B and across to D.

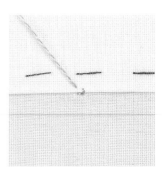

6 Pull the thread through firmly to open the holes. Completed first stitch.

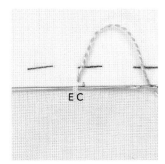

7 To begin the second stitch, take the needle to the back at C and re-emerge at E, a few fabric threads away from C.

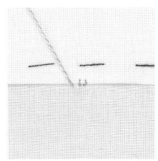

8 Pull the thread through.

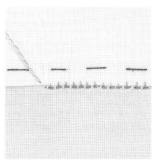

9 Repeat step 5. Pull the thread through firmly. Continue working stitches in this manner.

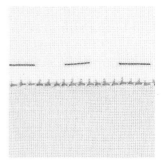

10 To end off, take the thread to the back and secure. Completed pin stitching.

MALTESE CROSS FILLING

Commonly known as Greek cross filling, this stitch is worked over an intersection of four by four threads. Work one quarter at a time, taking note of the number of wraps.

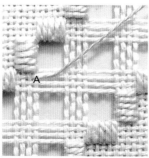

1 Bring the thread to the front at A.

2 Tightly wrap a pair of threads to B.

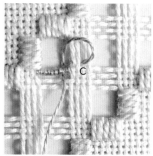

3 Bring the thread to the front at C. Take it back over the thread pair and under the wrapped threads.

4 Take the thread over the wrapped threads and under the unwrapped threads.

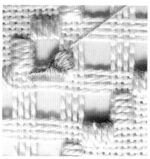

5 Continue working in a figure 8, easing the stitch tension to create a fan shape.

6 Wrap the remaining pair of threads back to the kloster block edge.

7 Repeat steps 1–4.

8 Repeat steps 5 and 6.

9 Repeat this sequence of stitching twice more to complete the Maltese cross.

MOUNTMELLICK STITCH

The appearance of this traditional stitch is easily altered by spacing the stitches further apart and extending the stitch to the side.

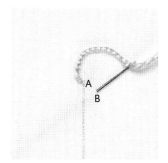

1 Emerge at A. Take the needle to the back at B, below and to the right of A.

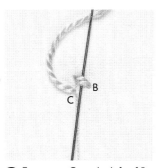

2 Emerge at C, to the left of B. Slide the needle downwards under the first stitch.

3 Pull the thread through. Loop the thread to the left and take the needle to the back at A.

4 Pull through, leaving a loop. Re-emerge at C, inside the thread loop.

5 Pull the thread through until the loop lies snugly against the emerging thread.

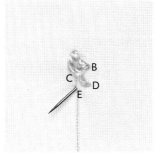

6 Take the thread to the back at D, below B, and emerge at E, below C.

7 Loop the thread to the left and slide the needle downwards under the second stitch.

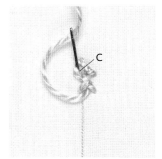

8 Pull through and loop the thread to the left. Take the needle to the back at C, inside the previous stitch.

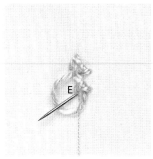

9 Pull through, leaving a loop. Re-emerge at E, inside the loop.

10 Pull the thread through until the loop lies snugly against the emerging thread.

11 Repeat steps 6–10 to the end of the row. Take the needle to the back just over the last loop.

NEEDLEWEAVING – FIVE STAGGERED RHOMBUS

Needleweaving is worked from the right side of the fabric. Each square on the stitch chart represents a drawn thread square on the shape. Here the needleweaving is worked over a base of single faggot stitch. Find the centre of the shape by counting the squares. The thread tail is left hanging at the front and will be secured later.

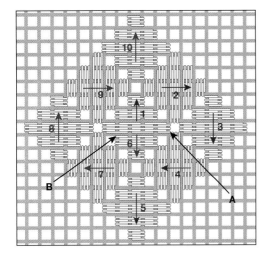

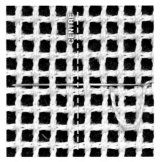

1 **Centre rhombus.** Beginning at the third square to the right of the centre, weave through the thread bundles from right to left under, over, three times.

2 Pull the thread through. Weave from left to right through the previous squares in the opposite order.

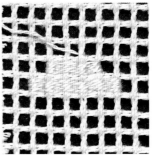

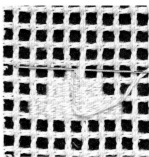

3 Continue weaving back and forth until you have woven three rows in each direction and the row of five squares is filled.

4 Take the needle to the back over the first thread bundle and emerge in the row above, one square closer to the centre.

5 Weave as before, filling only three squares instead of five. Take the needle to the back and emerge at the centre square.

6 Weave back and forth over the two thread bundles to fill the centre square and complete the upper half of the centre rhombus.

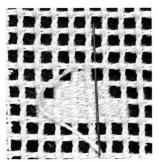

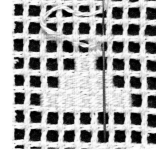

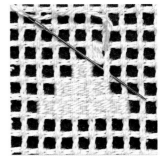

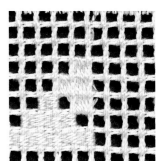

7 **Second rhombus.** Take the needle under the horizontal thread bundle on the right and emerge in next square above.

8 Working in a perpendicular direction to the previous stitching, weave to fill one square in the same manner as step 6.

9 Take the needle from left to right under the vertical thread bundle below.

10 With the needle tip pointing away from you, take the needle under the next horizontal thread bundle to the right. Continue weaving, filling three squares.

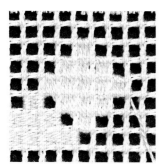

11 Continue weaving the rhombus shape over five, three and one square.

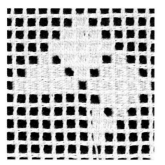

12 Continue working rhombus shapes alternating the weaving direction for each one.

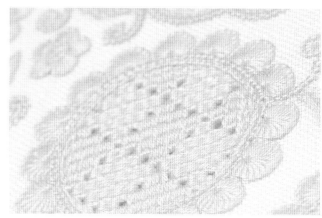

NEEDLEWOVEN BAR

Needlewoven bars are used to create the lace border and in groups of three to form the mesh in the centre square.

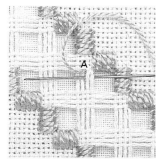

1 Bring the thread to the front at A. Take the needle around two threads and re-emerge at A.

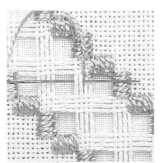

2 Tighten the stitch. Take the needle around the two threads on the left and come up through the centre.

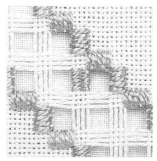

3 Tighten the stitch. Continue in this manner until the bar is filled with six stitches on each side.

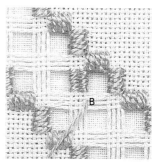

4 Carry the thread behind the fabric and bring to the front at B to begin the next bar.

OUTLINE STITCH

This stitch is worked in a similar way to stem stitch. In outline stitch, however, the thread is always kept above the needle, resulting in a smoother line than stem stitch.

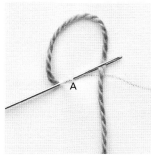

1 Emerge at the left-hand end of the design line. With the thread above the needle, take the needle to the back at A and emerge at the end.

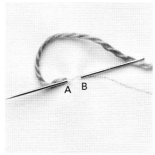

2 With the thread above the needle, take the needle from B to A, emerging through the same hole.

3 Continue working stitches in the same manner. Always keep the thread above the needle and the stitches the same length.

4 For the last stitch, take the thread to the back.

PADDED SATIN STITCH

A raised effect is achieved by filling the shape with straight stitches before working the satin stitch.

1 Using one strand, stitch around the outline of the shape in tiny split stitch.

2 Fill inside the shape with straight stitches worked very close together.

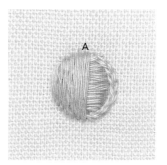

3 Beginning at A, bring the needle to the front just outside the split stitch outline. Work satin stitches in the opposite direction to the filling stitches.

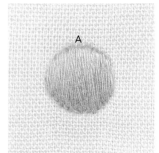

4 Working from A, fill in the remaining half of the shape. Completed padded satin stitch.

PART MALTESE CROSS / WRAPPING / BLANKET STITCH

We outlined the cut threads with kloster blocks to hold the cut fabric threads in place.

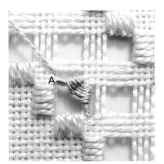

1 Work one quarter of Maltese cross filling in the same manner as before. Bring the needle to the front at A.

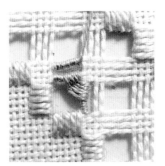

2 Tightly wrap the pair of threads to the thread intersection.

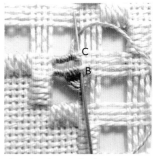

3 Take the needle from B to C, ensuring that the thread is under the needle tip.

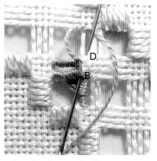

4 Take the needle from B to D, again ensuring that the thread is under the needle tip.

5 Continue working blanket stitch over the thread intersection and between each thread, always taking the needle to the back at B.

6 Slide the needle under the remaining pair of threads.

7 Wrap the threads back to the intersection.

8 Complete the row. Work a second row, offsetting it to the first, as shown.

PEAHOLE CORNER

Peahole hem corners are worked after mitreing the corners and securing the hem of a cloth.
Carefully mount each corner of the cloth in a hoop before working the embroidery.

1 Secure the thread at the back of several four-sided stitches close to the corner and emerge just above the last four-sided stitch.

2 Take the needle from right to left under the thread bundle closest to the corner.

3 Pull the thread taut. Take the needle from right to left diagonally under the intersecting thread bundles.

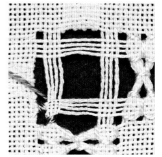

4 Pull the thread taut. Wrap the corner bundles twice more.

5 Keeping even tension, weave under and over the corner thread bundles for nine rows. Do not pull too tightly.

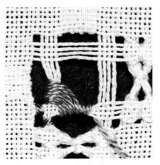

6 Wrap around the lower thread bundle twice more towards the inside corner.

7 Weave around the thread bundles at the new corner in the same manner as before.

8 Repeat steps 2–7 at each remaining corner. Secure the thread through the back of the weaving stitches and the four-sided stitches.

PEAHOLE HEM STITCH

This traditional Schwalm hem embroidery is worked between two rows of four-sided stitch on the outer edge of the cloth. The stitch is worked from corner to corner on the wrong side of the fabric.

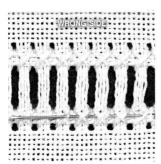

1 Secure the thread, sliding through the back of several four-sided stitches on the lower row.

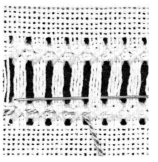

2 Take the needle from right to left under the first bundle of threads to the left.

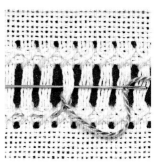

3 Pull the thread taut. Take the needle from right to left at the centre of the bundle.

4 Pull the thread taut. Take the needle from right to left through the back of the first two four-sided stitches above the bundle.

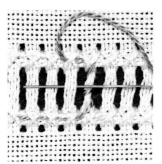

5 Pull the thread taut. Take the needle from right to left under the second thread bundle.

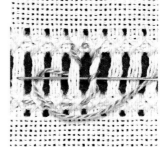

6 Take the needle from right to left under the first and second thread bundles keeping the thread under the tip of the needle.

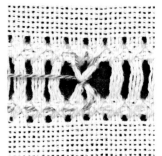

7 Pull the thread taut, pulling the thread bundles firmly together at the centre.

8 Take the needle from right to left under the lower half of the second thread bundle.

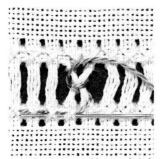

9 Take the needle from right to left through the back of the two, four-sided stitches below the second and third thread bundles.

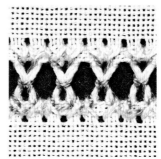

10 Continue steps 2–9 around the hem up to the next corner. Anchor the thread in the upper row of four-sided stitches to secure.

PORCUPINE STITCH

This stitch is formed by wrapping a straight stitch.

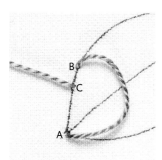

1 Bring the thread to the front at A. Take the needle to the back at B and emerge at C.

2 Pull the thread through. Wrap the long stitch by taking the thread over and under the stitch in a clockwise direction.

3 Pulling each wrap snugly, work a further 4–5 wraps. Take the needle to the back at A.

4 Repeat steps 1–3 to fill one half of the leaf, adjusting the spacing and direction of the stitches as required.

RAISED STEM STITCH BRANCH

The raised stem stitch is worked over a layer of padding formed with lengths of cotton perlé.
Fold the bundle in half to make twenty thicknesses. Contrasting threads have been used for clarity.

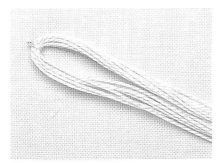

1 Secure the folded end of the threads to the top left-hand end of the marked line.

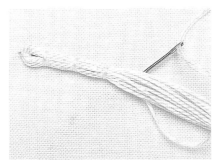

2 Couch the padding in place. Bring the needle up on marked line, take it over padding and then back through the same hole.

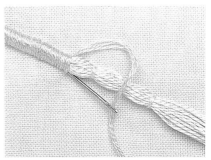

3 Work satin stitch over the padding, angling the needle under the padding.

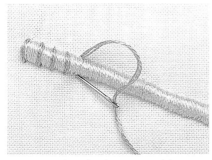

4 Create a base for the stem stitch by working a series of loose straight stitch bars at 2mm (1/16in) intervals.

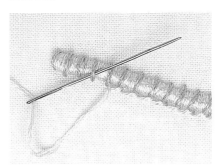

5 With three strands of stranded cotton in the tapestry needle, work stem stitch over the bars, beginning at the lower right-hand end.

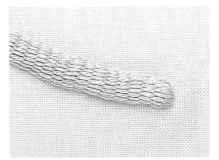

6 Begin each row at the same end, packing the rows firmly together.

RUNNING STITCH

Running stitch is quick and easy to work and is often used to form the foundation of other stitches
such as whipped running stitch and Holbein stitch. When working on plain weave fabrics,
make the stitch on the right side of the fabric slightly longer than the stitch on the wrong side.

1 Draw a line on the fabric. Bring the thread to the front on the right-hand end of the line.

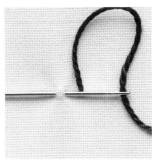

2 Take a small stitch, skimming the needle beneath the fabric along the line.

3 Pull the thread through. Take another stitch as before, ensuring the stitch is the same length as the previous stitch.

4 Continue in the same manner to the end of the row. Completed running stitch.

SATIN OUTLINE

Used in French whitework where it is known as cordonnet, satin outline is similar to trailing but is usually consistent in height and width, so there are no threads added or subtracted. It is worked along a single design line. When worked over a thicker line of stitching it is known as point de bourdon or bourdon stitch.

1 Secure the thread and bring it to the front at the beginning of the line.

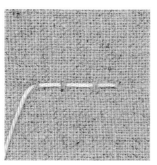

2 Work running stitches along the design line taking only 1–2 threads of fabric when making a stitch.

3 Continue working in this manner to the end of the line. You should have long stitches on the top of the fabric and tiny stitches on the back.

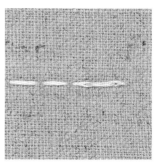

4 Bring the thread to the front at the centre of the first stitch. Take the thread to the back just before the centre of the second stitch, splitting the stitch.

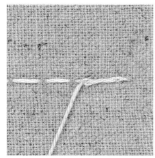

5 Bring the thread to the front just beyond the centre of the second stitch, again splitting the stitch. Pick up only 1–2 threads of fabric with this stitch.

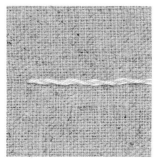

6 Repeat steps 4 and 5, working in this manner to the end of the line.

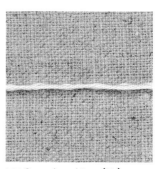

7 Cut a thread 5cm (2in) longer than the line. Ensure this 'guide' rests on top of the padding, without being attached, when working the satin stitch.

8 Beginning with a new thread, work satin stitches over the padding and guide, angling the needle as it passes through the fabric, to maintain a fine line.

SATIN STITCH BARS – DIAGONAL STEP

This stitch is used to fill the large leaves. To prepare the fabric, withdraw every fourth thread (cut one, leave three) both vertically and horizontally within the shape to form a grid.

1 **Right step.** Bring the thread to the front at the lower left of the shape (A). Take the needle to the back at B and emerge at C, one thread above A.

2 Repeat the previous step twice, moving up one thread each time and bringing the thread to the front at D after the last stitch.

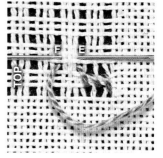

3 Pull the thread taut. Rotate the fabric 90 degrees to the left and take the needle from E to F.

4 Work two satin stitches parallel with the first stitch as before.

5 Rotate the fabric back and work three satin stitches over the next group of three fabric threads.

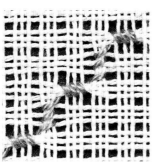

6 Continue in the same manner until the diagonal row is complete.

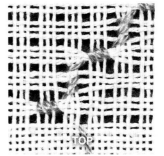

7 Turn the work upside down and bring the needle to the front one thread group below or to the right of the last block.

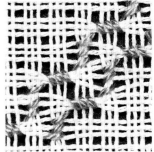

8 Work the next row in a similar manner to the first, alternating the vertical and horizontal bars.

SAWTOOTH BLANKET STITCH

Worked closely together this is a traditional border stitch for Mountmellick work.

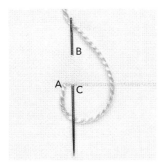

1 Bring the thread to the front at A. Take the needle the back at B, emerge at C with the thread under the needle tip.

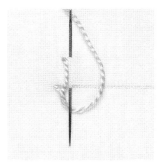

2 Pull the thread through and work a second stitch exactly the same as the first.

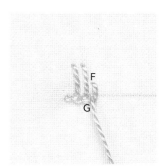

3 Take the needle to the back at F and emerge at G to make a short stitch.

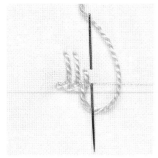

4 Work a second short stitch in the same manner.

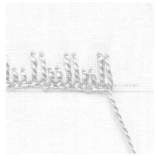

5 Continue working stitches in the same manner, always working two long and then two short stitches.

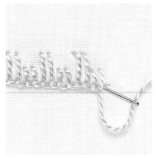

6 To finish, take the needle to the back of the fabric just over the last loop.

SEED STITCH

Seed stitch is excellent for adding textural interest to the surface of the fabric and for creating delicate shading. Seed stitches can be one, two or three stitches worked through the same holes in the same manner as backstitch. It is very important to maintain the correct pull on the thread so that each stitch retains its definition.

1 Bring the thread to the front at A at the right-hand end of the shape.

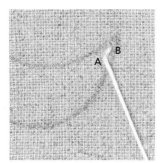

2 Take the needle to the back at B and emerge at A, ready to work the next stitch. Pull the thread firmly but do not distort the fabric.

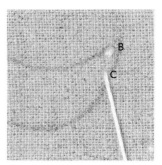

3 Take the needle to the back at B and emerge at C ready to work the next stitch.

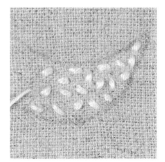

4 Continue working in this manner until the shape is filled.

SINGLE FAGGOT FILLING

This stitch is worked diagonally and opens out an evenly spaced grid of holes across the fabric. Work the first row across the widest point of the shape and fill to one side, then complete the remaining side.
Each row shares fabric holes with the previous row.
Each stitch is worked over four fabric threads.

1 **Row 1.** Emerge at A. Take the needle from B to C.

2 Pull the thread taut. Take the needle from A to D, four fabric threads to the left of B and C.

3 Pull the thread taut. Take the needle from C to E.

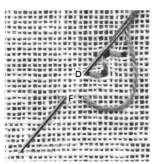

4 Pull the thread taut. Take the needle from D to F.

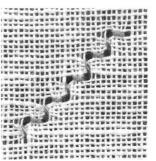

5 Pull the thread taut. Repeat the stitch sequence to the end of the row.

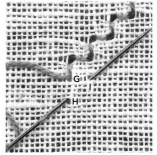

6 **Row 2.** Emerge at G. Take the needle from H to I.

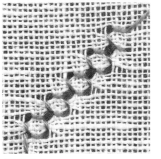

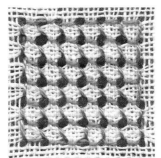

7 Pull the thread taut. Take the needle through the holes created by the previous row as shown.

8 Pull the thread taut. Continue working stitches in the same manner along the diagonal, in the opposite direction to row 1.

9 Continue working diagonal rows of single faggot filling to complete the shape, working partial rows where needed.

SINGLE FAGGOT STITCH

This stitch is used to reinforce the fabric grid before working any further decorative stitches on large shapes, or as a decorative stitch on its own for smaller shapes.

Prepare the grid by withdrawing pairs of vertical and horizontal fabric threads (cut two, leave two). Rotate the fabric so the thread grid is on the diagonal and work the stitch across the grid from right to left on the wrong side.

1 Take the needle through the first hole near the right-hand edge at the widest section of the shape (A) and emerge at the next hole to the left (B).

2 Pull the thread through. Take the needle from C to D on the diagonal line below.

3 Pull the thread through. Take the needle from B to E on the first diagonal line.

4 Pull the thread through. Continue this sequence to the opposite side of the shape and secure thread on outer edge.

5 Turn the work upside down. Beginning on the first completed row, work a second row in the same manner as the first.

6 Continue working rows in the same manner across the shape, one half at a time, turning the fabric as required.

SQUARE EYELET

This stitch can be combined with double bar satin stitch blocks. To prepare the fabric, withdraw every fourth thread (cut one, leave three) both vertically and horizontally within the shape to form a grid.

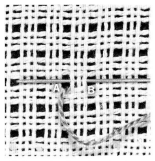

1 Bring the thread to the front at A. Take the needle from B to A.

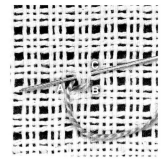

2 Pull the thread taut. Take the needle from C, one fabric thread above B, to A.

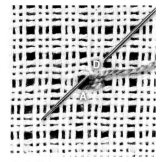

3 Pull the thread taut. Take the needle from D, one fabric thread above C, to A.

4 Pull the thread taut. Work further stitches one fabric thread apart, counter-clockwise, returning to the centre for each stitch.

5 Work the last stitch over the first stitch. Take the needle from B to E, three thread groups above.

6 Pull the thread through. Work a second square eyelet as before.

7 Stitch the following rows in a similar manner to form a chequered pattern.

STEM STITCH

The thread is always kept below the needle. The length of the stitches may vary depending on the type of thread used and the look you wish to achieve.

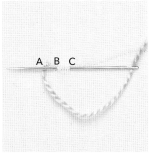

1 Bring the thread to the front at A. Lay the thread below the marked line. Take the needle from C to B. The needle always goes through the fabric on the marked line.

2 Pull the thread through. Take the needle from D to C keeping the thread below the needle.

3 Continue in the same manner ensuring the needle emerges at beginning of the previous stitch.

4 To end off, take the needle to the back and secure the thread. Completed stem stitch.

TRELLIS COUCHING

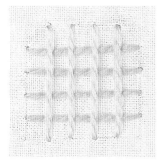

1 Mark the shape on the fabric and fill with a grid of straight stitches using the first thread.

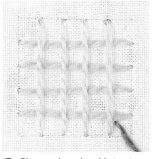

2 Change thread and bring it to the front in the lower left corner of one intersection.

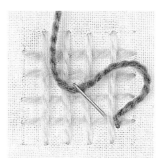

3 Take the needle to the back in the upper right corner, just over the straight stitches.

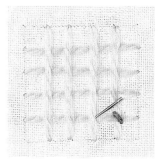

4 Pull the thread through. Emerge in the lower left corner of the next intersection.

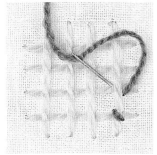

5 Pull the thread through. Take the needle to the back in the upper right corner, just over the straight stitches.

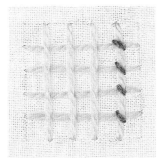

6 Pull the thread through. Continue in the same manner across the row.

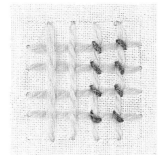

7 Work back across the next row, ensuring the couching stitches lie in the same direction as those of the first row.

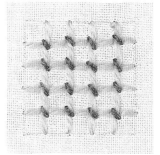

8 Work all remaining rows in the same manner. End off on the back of the fabric.

WAFFLE FILLING

Worked in a similar manner to honeycomb filling, waffle filling omits the horizontal backstitches, resulting in a flowing, wave-like texture. The tension of the pulled stitching causes the vertical stitches to lie on the diagonal. Each stitch is worked over four fabric threads.

1 Beginning at the right-hand side, emerge at A. Take the needle from B to C.

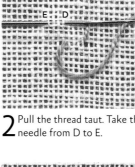

2 Pull the thread taut. Take the needle from D to E.

3 Pull the thread taut. Take the needle from F to G.

4 Pull the thread taut. Repeat the stitch sequence across the row.

5 Turn the work 180°. Stitch the second row as a mirror image to the first.

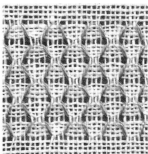

6 Continue working rows across the fabric in the same manner to fill the shape.

WAVE STITCH

This stitch is used to fill the centre petal of the large tulip. It creates a delicate lacy effect with zigzag stitches joining tiny regular holes in the fabric. The stitches are worked from right to left as closely as possible to the border so that the chain stitches look as though they are lying on top of the filling pattern. To prepare the fabric withdraw every fourth horizontal thread (cut one, leave three) within the shape.

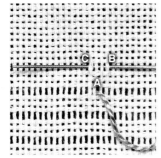

1 **Row 1.** Bring the thread to the front at A. Take the needle to back at B on the drawn line above and two threads to the right of A. Emerge at C four threads to the left.

2 Pull the thread taut. Take the needle back through A and pick up four threads to the left. Emerge at D.

3 Pull the thread taut. Take the needle from C to E, picking up four threads as before.

4 Pull the thread taut. Repeat steps 2 and 3 until reaching the left-hand side of the shape.

5 **Row 2.** Take the needle from F on the upper line to G on the drawn line below row 1.

6 Turn the work upside down. Take the needle from right to left through the holes of the last wave stitch on row 1.

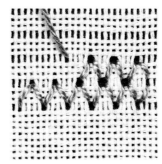

7 Continue working wave stitches across the row in the same manner as before.

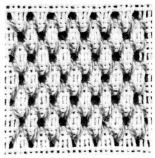

8 Work the third and following rows in the same manner to fill the shape.

There's more
to explore...